TERRORISM TORTURE AND TEACHING

THE EFFECTS OF VIOLENCE ON THE EDUCATION OF WOMEN

Dear Timmy Best
Thank you so much
for your books
and support
I remain grateful
and appreciative
of your support.
(AWOKU!)
Fr Vincent Burke
11/11/2021

TERRORISM TORTURE AND TEACHING

THE EFFECTS OF VIOLENCE ON THE EDUCATION OF WOMEN

VINCENT HASSAN BULUS, PH.D

TERRORISM, TORTURE AND TEACHING
The Effects of Violence on the Education of Women

Published by Krystal Lee Enterprises (KLE Publishing)

Edited by LM Editing
Graphics by Harrison Forde
Formatted for print by Kensington Type & Graphics

Please send comments and questions:
Krystal Lee Enterprises LLC
www.KLEPub.com 770-240-0089 Ext. 1
klepublishing@gmail.com or sales@klepub.com
Printed in the United States of America.
ISBN: 978-1-945066-02-3

This book is dedicated to my mother, Lalai Angelina, and father, Bulus Kurah Kantiok Duniya, for their love and teaching us the value of human dignity and peaceful coexistence.

Foreword

Terrorism and its variants have been a significant feature on the landscape of politics among nations and communities across the world. In our times, the world has witnessed a global wave of unprecedented terrorism, often assuming menacing proportions and brutal dimensions.

In practice, it is deliberate, calculated, and targeted, often with an accompanying ideology that is, at best, without a clear perception of goals and objectives. These undefined goals are often antithetical and inimical to the authority of the Nation State. Over the years, the international community, especially the United Nations (U.N.) Security Council Resolutions, has made determined attempts to address these perilous threats to peace and security through concerted action.

The broader threats of terrorism manifest in homegrown violence and intimidation, which then spreads with transnational tentacles. Thus, its reach far exceeds the abiding domestic threat to the security, prosperity, and economic well-being of the Nation State.

In Sovereign States where domestic terrorists have established both a presence and influence, they engage in practices that undermine and impede the advance ment of education, especially for female children. In the midst of the violence, girls attend school at considerable risk, while their parents become increasingly hesitant to allow them to participate. The consequence of this reluctance is the loss of inspiration to empower their children through education.

In this seminal study, Dr. Vincent Bulus Hassan reveals the threat of Domestic Terrorism as a clear and present danger to the education of the "girl-child" in Northern Nigeria. As a professional educator, who prizes education as the undeniable path to development, Dr, Bulus draws a vivid portrait of the critical role of the girl-child in our era with the perils of Domestic Terrorism at its center. His perspectives on Domestic

Terrorism and the consequences for the girl-child and national development convey an unequivocal message to state actors that nations face a collective threat and danger to advancement .

The reverberations of these threats are quite compelling. I believe that this will inspire Statesmen and women and citizens alike to muster all-hands-on-deck. This implies that genuine, international cooperation constitutes the key to effectively confront a threat that cannot be dealt with exclusively at the domestic level. Thus, this study is a critically important addition to the burgeoning literature on Domestic dimension of Terrorism.

U. Joy Ogwu
Professor of Political Science & International Relations
Nigerian Institute of International Affairs

Contents

SECTION ONE

Conceptual Clarification of Terrorism: Girl-child Education and Sundry Issues

One critical, analytical problem with understanding crises in the Northern region of Nigeria is finding appropriate concepts to explain the insurgents' activities. Some see the crises as terrorism, criminality, ritual activities, ethno-religious militarism, rebellion, freedom fighting, revolutionaries and/or a combination of political agitations. The manifestations of these armed groups constitute, what is referred to as, Domestic Terrorism, which are directly linked to unresolved conflicts in Nigeria and the failure of its government to gain control of rebellious foes in the region.

Northern Nigeria is a region with many security problems. Identifying the security predicament of the region according to its different blocs, Okoli (2021) says that chief among the security problems is the Islamic militant group's (popularly known as Boko Haram) insurgency in the Northeast. In the North-central region, herdsmen militancy has become a key security concern while the Northwest, which used to be the bastion of security and stability, has been hit hard by banditry. This suggests that Northern Nigeria is bleeding from all sides as a result of violent conflicts by non-state actors that are multiplying in numbers and wreaking havoc of unimaginable dimension.

In this book, my basic concern is to examine the activities of one of the non-state actors, the Boko Haram, and its impact on girl-child education in Northern Nigeria. This dreaded group has since been classified as terrorists. In order to provide a context for this conversation, it is proper that some key concepts constituting the framework of this discourse be explained.

CHAPTER ONE
Terrorism

It is important to say from the outset that there is no universally agreed upon definition of terrorism. Furthermore, Laqueur (1976, 6) observes that despite its historical dimension, terrorism is a relatively recent concept. The term "Terrorism" first appeared in the 1798 Dictionnaire de l'Academie Française as a "systeme, regime de la terreur" and was used by the Jacobins to refer to themselves with positive connotation. It was only after the 9th of Thermidor that it assumed a negative value, becoming synonymous with criminal intent.

Abimbola and Adesote (2016) say that the first known acts of what we now call terrorism were perpetrated by a radical offshoot of the Zealots, a Jewish sect active in Judea during the 1st century AD. The Zealots resisted the Roman Empire's rule of today's Israel through a determined campaign primarily involving assassination.

Despite the complexity and political weight of any definitions of terrorism (Jackson et al. 2011), generally speaking, it understood to be "the deliberate creation and exploitation of fear through violence or the threat of violence in the pursuit of political change" (Hoffman 1998, 32). More specifically, it is argued that terrorism "embodies the exerting and implementing of power, and the attempted redressing of power relations; it represents a subspecies of warfare, and as such it can form part of a wider campaign of violent and non-violent attempts at political leverage" (English 2009, 24).

Many consider terrorism as the intentional striking of fear, anxiety and intimidation into a target population to achieve a political objective (Schmid and Jongman, 2017, Wilkinson et al, 2003, Kilcullen, 2005). Additionally, terrorism is the unlawful use or threatened use of force or violence against individuals or property in an attempt to coerce by intimidating governments or societies to achieve political, religious or ideological objectives (Johnston). It is argued that such a broad conceptual framework logically applies to such a diverse range of phenomena as to be counterproductive. These phenomena include jihadist groups, organized crime networks, hate criminality and even institutionalized violence against women.

Others, such as Kiras (2007), have also identified a state's monopoly on violence as an implicitly terroristic threat. Concurrently, however, terrorism has evolved into a highly politicized term applied to any methods that seem to defy public morality. It retains the post-colonial stigma of being an 'ungentlemanly' way of war, with the implication that an actor thus identified is either irrational, illegitimate or simply 'beyond the pale' (Kilcullen, 2005).

However, terrorism is generally defined as politically motivated violence by clandestine groups or individuals against civilians or non-combatant personnel. Thus, terrorism is, by nature, political because it involves the acquisition and use of power for the purpose of forcing others to submit, or agree, to terrorist demands. Legal statutes in most countries around the world regard terrorism as a crime. Yet, there is considerable variation in how these laws define terrorism, even in countries whose laws derive from a common origin.

In the United Kingdom, for example, legislation titled, Terrorist Act 2000 (Encarta 2009), states that terrorism is the use or threat of action designed to influence the government or intimidate the public or a section of the public for the purpose of advancing a political, religious or ideological cause. The Encarta (2009) also points out that the United States Department of State has adopted the definition found in Title 22 of the United States federal code, which calls terrorism "premeditated, politically motivated violence perpetrated against non-combatant targets by sub-national groups or clandestine agents, usually intended to influence an audience."

It is important to mention that the purpose of this research is not to offer an objective or scientific definition of terrorism. By referring to terrorist groups, I consider their basic tactical strategy choices, their use of terror as a tool of warfare and an instrument to gain political visibility. So conceived, I underline the political dimension to distinguish mere criminal acts from those of terrorism, which involve bombings, assassinations, hijackings, hostage taking, and other violence, in order to intimidate nations into changing their policies or their leaders into surrendering parts of their territory.

Terrorism hurts all nations – large and small, rich and poor. It takes a toll on human beings of every age and income, culture and religion. It strikes against everything.

It is emphasized that terrorism is divided into two categories – Domestic and International. This means that if an Israeli insurgent kidnaps and kills an American Ambassador, it is an act of international terrorism. While at the same time, if the attack is targeted on Israeli government officials, it is domestic terrorism. However, if an Israeli bombs an Israeli Embassy in any country outside Israel, it is still considered domestic terrorism. Therefore, Ojukwu (2011) observes that the kidnapping of government officials and other Nigerians, bombing of oil companies, pipeline destruction by the militants in the Niger Delta region, and the recent bombings in the Northern part of Nigeria by Boko Haram is also domestic terrorism.

David (2016) says that terrorism, which had been viewed by some members of the general public as a predominantly Western narrative and, supposedly, Western conundrum, has become a Nigerian issue fomented by some Nigerians to express their grievances. Bockstette (2008) sees terrorism as political violence in an asymmetrical conflict designed to induce terror and incite fear (sometimes indiscriminate) through the violent victimization and destruction of non-combatant targets, involving acts meant to send a message from an illicit clandestine organization. He argues further that the purpose of terrorism is to exploit the media in order to achieve maximum attainable publicity as an amplifying multiplier in order to influence the targeted audience and reach short- and mid-term political goals and/or desired long-term purposes.

Schmidt and Youngman (1988) cite 109 different definitions of terrorism, which they obtained in a survey of leading academics. From these definitions, they isolated the following recurring elements in order of their statistical appearance in the definitions:

- Violence, force (83.5%)
- Political (65%)
- Fear, emphasis on terror (51%)
- Threats (47%)
- Psychological effects and anticipated reactions (41.5%)
- Discrepancy between the targets and victims (37.5%)
- Intentional, planned, systematic, organized action (32%)
- Methods of combat, strategy, and tactics (30.5%)

Kydd and Walter (2006) reveal that there are five principal strategies of terrorism.

1. **Attrition** – persuasion by the enemy imposing considerable cost/ damage
2. **Intimidation** – convincing the population that they are stronger than the government
3. **Provocation** – triggering the enemy to respond in indiscriminate violence
4. **Spoiling** – undermining the attempts to reach a peace settlement
5. **Outbidding** – using violence to convince people that they are worthy of support.

Nigerians have experienced *all* the strategies playing out.

Meanwhile, Nigeria's security crisis and challenges can be traced to its geographical, political, and economic circumstances. The very nature of the country's economic, political and structural relations breeds fractious inequality and marginalization of the bulk of Nigerians, though not the causes, they are the most basic motivations for terrorism.

In critical terrorism studies, scholars, such as Sagir (2017), who are mostly realist discuss how once a government deprives or fails to provide the basics of life, such as security, education, employment and health services, to their citizens, the citizens, out of the critical condition, could resort to extra means to the extent of challenging the state's legitimacy and its exclusive monopoly of the instruments of violence.

Don (2013) implies that, given the complexity of the security situation in Nigeria, blended with the economic, political and social strife, projects and programs designed to counter terrorism should be built around community resilience against terrorism, and cooperation among law enforcement agencies and strengthening judicial institutions must be enhanced. Hence, strategy and the importance of collective efforts to counter terrorism in an increasingly interdependent and interconnected fashion have become imperative for Nigeria.

The following are several highlighted measures used for counter-terrorism in Nigeria. Each of these initiatives targets a different aspect of what Piombo (2017) calls "the four Ds" of fighting terrorism.

1. Defeat terrorists and their organizations
2. Deny sponsorship, support and sanctuary to terrorists
3. Diminish the underlying conditions that terrorist seek to exploit
4. Defend citizens and interests at home and abroad

The counter-terrorism measures proposed include the Meghalaya Model, a multi-sector approach involving government, law enforcement, judiciary and civil society organizations, initially used in North East Asia in 1999, which created a comprehensive framework for combating trafficking under "the five Ps" – Prevention, Protection, Policing, Press and Prosecution (Kharbhih, (2010). The Meghalaya Model is designed to track and rescue trafficked children then facilitate rehabilitation and ensure survivors do not get re-trafficked. It also provides families with livelihood alternatives, evidence to prosecute offenders, and raises awareness through the media. Additionally, the Meghalaya Model process uses "the five Rs" – Reporting, Rescue, Rehabilitation, Repatriation and Re-education.

These pillars of the Meghalaya Model to counter human trafficking are relevant to counter terrorism as they could combat the supply of terrorists and mercenaries for terrorism as well as the demand for terrorist networks. This is imperative because, despite international agreements and an excess of national laws on counter-terrorism, it remains one of the fastest growing criminal activities in the world due to its cross border nature, which requires cooperation and collaboration between countries if it is to be tackled effectively.

The Meghalaya Model, though originally designed to track and rescue trafficked children, could be adopted or adapted to counter terrorism in Nigeria as there are insinuations of mercenaries and conscripted fighters for Boko Haram terrorists. Coupled with the loose nature of Nigerian borders and rate of human trafficking in the country, these mercenaries and conscripted fighters could easily be trafficking victims from neighboring countries.

CHAPTER TWO
Girl-child Education

The term girl-child seems to have emerged in the broader public discourse in the late 1980s when United Nation Children Education Fund (UNICEF) adopted it as a primary focus. Subsequently, the United Nations proclaimed 1990 "The Year of the Girl-Child" and the 1990s "The Decade of the Girl-Child" (Berman et al, 2002). At the U.N. Fourth World Conference on Women in Beijing in 1995, the plight of the girl-child was a key topic area, resulting in a platform for action with nine strategic objectives, including the elimination of all forms of discrimination against the girl-child, the eradication of violence against the girl-child, and the promotion and protection of the rights of the girl-child (United Nations, 1995).

The term girl-child is popular, especially among development scholars and other social scientists with varying age ranges. Mukhtar et al (2011) cited by Mvendaga et al (2014) refers to the term girl-child as a female between the ages of 6-18 years. Ada (2001) defines the girl-child as a female below 14 years of age where Offorma (2009) describes a girl-child as a biological female offspring from birth to eighteen (18) years old, the age before one becomes a young adult. This period covers the crèche, nursery or early childhood (0 – 5 years), primary (6 – 12 years) and secondary school (12 – 18 years).

Despite the differences in span, all involve a period where the young child is totally under the care of an adult (parents, guardians, or older siblings) and malleable, building and developing her personality and character. She is very dependent on the significance of others, those on whom she models her behavior whether it be through observation, repetition or imitation. Her physical, mental, social, spiritual and emotional developments begin in this period and progress to the peak at the young adult stage.

According to Peters and Akpan (2017), there have been distracting facts of segregation, neglect and cultural clamp over the education of the girl-child, especially in the

Northern region of Nigeria. According to Education for All's (EFA) Global Monitoring Report 2012, 10.5 million Nigerian children are not attending school. In 2019, Northern Nigeria harbored the highest number of school age children in the world that were out of school. In some states in the federation, enrollment of children in schools is as low as 12.0% and 6 of the 36 million girls not in school world-wide are Nigerians. The global figure for out of school children is estimated at 121 million, 65 million are girls with over 80 percent of these girls in sub-Saharan Africa, including Nigeria (UNICEF, 2007).

Andrew and Etumabo (2016) say that girl-child education is a catch-all term for a complex set of issues and debates surrounding girls and women, particularly primary, secondary, tertiary and health education. Education is a responsibility that naturally forms part of human life. It propels human adaptation to the environment through observation, traditions and customs that are fortified within an organized environment called "school." Denying the girl-child access to education implies making her a dysfunctional member of the society.

Peters and Akpan (2017) say that, naturally, from the formative years of childhood, education has its foundation from the family (the home). As babies, when carried by their mothers, lullabies are sung to calm the sucking urge of the child. While working and involved in home chores, traditional songs are rendered by mothers, siblings, and babysitters to ease boredom and lighten burdens. This continues to a time when the child associates with the playmates and interacts with the immediate environment, culminating in a fundamental development and expansion of the child's sense of comprehension.

It is at this juncture that the origin all mental dispositions in humankinds are formed. For every human being the first educational exercise begins with the mother who, at one time in her life, was a girl-child herself. As the girl-child is the root executor of the first basic, though informal, educational principles, every human empowerment should be given to her; that which can facilitate her home activities, guide her marital experiences and nurture her childcare.

It is only wise and inevitable that the girl-child is allowed to acquire an education that can equip her with all necessary tools for the successful execution of life. From the tender, cradle phases of humanity to a period when initiatives and other decisions can be injected into adult-life, education is an umbrella of skills and repertoire of organized ideas and ideals, which, as stressed by Okocha (2009), are a facet concerned more with practical work leading to acquisition of a particular occupation or career.

Education generally concerns itself with the imparting of knowledge to people.

Alabi and Alabi (2013) observe that knowledge, in this case, can be seen as the corpus of instruction and social ethos, hinging on the acquisition of abstract ideas, to refine the mind and acquisition of psycho-motor skills, which, in turn, makes for a skilled person or, at a minimum, positions one in the right frame of mind to acquire the skill necessary for existence in an atomized social order. Thus, education is, first and foremost, an imperative social tool for the continued survival and growth of human society.

Against this background, education, whether formal or informal, assumes a heavy social context. It is easy to figure out that the lack of social contextualization of education may be responsible for the inability of education to foster genuine development in many developing societies. It is not surprising that Oladosu (2007) expressed dissatisfaction at the predominance of conservative, rationalizing, romantic and democratic thoughts on education. He sees these as too retrogressive and inane to lead to a groundswell of activities and thought processes necessary for continued progress in any society.

Oladosu (2007) considers sustainable or progressive education as one containing the following criteria:

- Stressing the development of critical reasoning in the individual, a questioning attitude towards all existing reality - opposing the conservative tradition;
- Embodying a full acceptance of the social character of man, rejecting forever the notion of a pre-social dimension of human existence – opposing romantic schools of thought;
- Insisting on the active nature of the child's participation in the learning process and contrasting the mechanistic conception of education as the transmission of fixed skills – opposing rationalizers;
- Encouraging dialectic thought and discussion – opposing democratic tradition.

Many factors revolving around cultural and socio-economic experiences are associated with girl-child educational set-back. At many traditional levels, it is believed better for the woman to stay at home and learn how to care and manage her family instead of being in school. According to Denga (1993), it is a very prominent cultural view that has prevailed over the vicinities of most local homes. This traditional ideology largely contributes to preventing women from having adequate access to education.

To explain the fact that more boys than girls participated in education, Obasi (1997) identified a host of constraints, with "the Nigerian tradition" being named as top in the list. Nigerian tradition attaches higher value to a man than to a woman, whose place is believed to be in the home. A study by the University of Ibadan linked the imbalance in boys' and girls' participation in schooling to the long-held belief in male superiority and female subordination. This situation was further aggravated by patriarchal practices, which gave girls no traditional rights to succession. The same patriarchal practices encouraged preference to be given to the education of a boy rather than a girl.

In addition to the challenges therein, Peters and Akpan (2017) are of the view that education has become a luxury to many Nigerians, especially in the rural areas, due to a decline in economic activities. Families are highly influenced by birth order, sex, natural endowment or creative power. Even for Nigerian parents who may not subscribe to traditional gender roles, too often, the family can only afford to sponsor one child in school. Because a daughter has assumed responsibilities in the home, she is less likely to be the one to attend school.

According to Peters and Akpan (2017), all these effects are traceable to the beginning of colonialism and Christianity, where rigid ideas and ideals about gender perceptions were imposed on the African mind. There, the woman's role became traditionally limited to satisfying sexual needs of men, sexual and commercial labor, carrying loads, tending to children and home chores, like preparing food. The idea of "domesticity and housewife stigma" provided the springboard for which the girl-child educational imbalance came to manifest. They also observed that other cultural practices that have formed a negative enigma to women's growth and continually studded the emancipation of women to stardom include early forced marriage, widowhood practices, which also co-opts wife-inheritance, as well as submission to traditional superstition with questionable norms and principles.

In a nutshell, the overview of girl-child disparity with the boy-child, and the general stigma of regarding the woman as subordinate and a lesser personality in strength and academic disposition are mere human developments that subject our ideology to this imbalance in educational accessibility across gender categories.

The foregoing scholars and their various views regarding the challenge confronting girl-child education are apt but still ignore the role of violent conflict. This is unacceptable considering the avalanche of evidence that suggests a strong connection between violent conflict and the lack of access to education by the girl-child. This explains why DFID (2005) says violent conflict hurts girls most. DFID (2005) explains further that girls are particularly vulnerable to abuse and unequal access to schooling in fragile States suffering from conflict, lack of resources and/or people, high levels of corruption, and political instability.

What sets these countries apart is their failure to deliver on the core functions of government, including keeping people safe, managing the economy, and delivering basic services. This leads to violence and disease, as well as illiteracy and economic weakness, which are more prominent in these areas.

Of the 121 million children not in primary school globally, an estimated 37 million of them live in fragile States. Many of these children are girls. Girls' absence from school may be due to fears of violence or the reliance on their role as caregivers in the family. For girls who have been victims of violence in conflict situations, trauma can impair their ability to learn as well.

In summary, the girl-child in Nigeria, from a historical, social and economic viewpoint, has unequal access to education in relation to her male-child counterpart. This inequality could be due to the early sex role of the girls, which influence the conceptualization of their later status, and occupational inclination. In most cultures in Nigeria, the female-child played a subordinate role to the male child and is neglected right from birth. Adamu (2005) views the neglect of girl-child education as something that has to do with culture and religion, but Rufai (1996) attributes the neglect to various myths. Some of these include unfounded cultural beliefs that educated female children do not make submissive wives, they are promiscuous and/or often barren, and carry attitudes that are incompatible with their traditionally expected roles as future wives and mothers.

Umar (1996), states that female children, particularly in Northern Nigeria, are made to believe that their place as women is in the kitchen. Therefore, at home, she is socialized into accepting her traditional role of bearing and rearing children while also maintaining the welfare of her family. As far as parents are concerned, there is no need for female children to be prepared beyond attaining such traditional roles of being mothers and wives. It can be understood that this restricted view of female child education resulted in a persistent, lukewarm attitude towards exposing female children to Western education in the Northern part of the country.

The concern of this paper is that, despite the campaign by the Nigerian Federal Government, UNICEF, and academic stakeholders seeking to improve girl-child education in Nigeria, the level of discrimination is still high. Based on this, UNICEF has advocated for investment in girls' education as a means of allowing all children to fulfill their rights to quality education. Getting girls involved in school would counter all barriers that are currently keeping children out of school.

CHAPTER THREE

Locating Northern Nigeria

The amalgamation of Northern and Southern protectorates of what came to be known as Nigeria in 1914 remains a watershed. Before then, different parts of the country were living on their own with their varying administrative structures.

Northern Nigeria, for example, had its long tradition of the emirate system. Providing graphic possibilities of Northern Nigeria, Hoffman (2014) says that it is an area rich in natural solid minerals and agricultural potential. It is home to around 60% of the country's population, covering nearly two-thirds of Nigeria's land mass – approximately 711,828 square kilometers – and is twice the size of Germany. Until the first cycle of state creation in 1967, this area was officially designated the Northern Region.

However, the history of Nigeria's regions and states is sensitive and complex, making the current classification of 19 of the 36 federal states as 'Northern', specifically those lying in the middle of the country, not without contention. The inclusion of the region's southernmost parts under the Northern label has periodically been resisted by the mostly non-Hausa communities living there.

There is a preference for the term 'Middle-Belt' to describe the area that runs from Kwara through the federal capital, Abuja, down to Benue state (Hoffman, 2014). Geo-politically, Northern Nigeria is subdivided into Northeast (where Boko Haram formally held sway), North-central (where Fulani herdsmen are killing Christian farmers), and Northwest (where bandits have turned the area into a killing field).

Most research findings suggest that the Hausa, Fulani and Kanuri are the largest groups in Northern Nigeria and predominantly Muslim. The Muslim population is concentrated in the far northern states, but significant numbers of Christians also reside in this area as well. There are about 160 smaller ethnic groups across northern Nigeria that are mainly Christian along with a considerable percentage that follow traditional religious practices.

A study by Hoffman (2014) confirms that Northern Nigeria continues to display some of the worst human development indicators in the world. For instance, in Northeast Nigeria, 71.5% of the population live in absolute poverty, and more than half are malnourished, making it the poorest part of the country. Insecurity, desertification and flooding have interrupted farming activities, the main source of income for most Northerners. Less than 40% of Nigerian children, aged 6–11, attend any primary school, and it is Northern Nigeria that has the worst school attendance rates, especially among girls.

Furthermore, the literacy rate is 92% in Lagos, Nigeria's bustling commercial capital, while in Kano, the North's commercial capital and Nigeria's second biggest city, it is 49%. In the Northeastern state of Borno, the epicentre of the Boko Haram insurgency, it is under 15%. Additionally, Hoffman (2014) reveals that in 2010, nine of the 19 Northern states had the highest levels of unemployment in Nigeria – some as high as 40% – with young Northerners being overwhelmingly more likely to be jobless.

The worsening challenges of poverty, youth unemployment, poor infrastructure, illiteracy and insecurity are inherently systemic and a consequence of the collective failure of leaders at all tiers of government to properly deliver public goods and services or accountably manage public funds.

It is important to mention that Islam was embedded in Northern Nigeria for centuries before it rapidly spread south following the early 19th-century Islamic jihad of Uthman dan Fodio (1754 –1817), a Fulani Islamic scholar, who went on to establish the famous Sokoto Caliphate, Africa's largest independent polity. From the time of its inception, the caliphate, which consisted of autonomous emirates, consolidated its political control in many parts of Northern Nigeria through Islamic values and practices. During this era, power was primarily legitimized by religious authority. The older Kanem-Borno Empire in the Northeast was weakened by the political rise of Sokoto, but it resisted total domination. This was, however, at the cost of its leaders being excluded from emerging Islamic networks of power.

The opposition of the Kanuri in the Northeast to subjugation under Sokoto shaped the relationship between both power structures and is an important backdrop for understanding the violent contestation for control over Northeast Nigeria. During the 100-year existence of the caliphate, the hegemony of the Fulani ruling class and its interactions with the local Hausa aristocracy laid the groundwork for their combined political domination of northern Nigeria. This set of power relations remained after the defeat of the Sokoto caliphate by the British and was, in fact, further strengthened under colonialism.

By 1903 the takeover of the Sokoto caliphate was complete. Its well-established administrative structures were repurposed and progressively standardized to facilitate the British colonial policy of indirect rule. For this to work, the status of local traditional elites was invested with formal and legal authority while the colonial state drew upon their social and religious legitimacy. Although colonial arrangements narrowed the influence of traditional religious authority in Northern Nigeria – eventually limiting Islamic law to only civil matters – the delicate balance of indirect rule was dependent on this layer of authority staying in place.

This accommodation had an important impact on non-Hausa-Fulani, non-Muslim communities in the region, which had long struggled to assert their independence and distinctiveness in the face of emirate power. For these smaller, politically constrained groups, colonial rule had the unintended consequence of driving up conversions to Christianity, which could be interpreted as an expression of protest against the reinforcement of emirate administration. At the same time, it encouraged the suppression of non-Hausa-Fulani cultural identities so much that, when Nigeria became independent in 1960, the Hausa language, political culture and values had been widely assimilated by minority groups but so, too, was the fear of continued marginalization in a self-governing Nigeria. The swell of contemporary demands and competing claims to political autonomy, economic rights and opportunities from various communities in Northern Nigeria has its roots in this fraught past.

Similarly, within the Northern Muslim community, internal disagreements produced divisions between groups aligned with the two-centuries-strong Sufi heritage of the Sokoto caliphate and those who held a range of hardline to moderate 'reformist' views. This led to the exclusion of Muslim leaders and groups that fell into the latter category from local mainstream power structures. Even though over time some 'reformist' elements were co-opted and absorbed into the established system of religious and political authority, others who maintained their dissension were systematically pushed out to the sidelines and rendered politically voiceless.

The layers of political, social, religious and even doctrinal grievances produced during these successive phases still impact upon present-day power relations in Northern Nigeria and have been heavily appropriated in the past three decades of ethnic and faith-based political identity conflicts in the region.

For the "Middle Belt" of Northern Nigeria, Gudaku (2020) warns that the region has been very nebulous, and thus highly controversial to identify. To this extent, Gaya (2002, p. 14) argues that "the scope and meaning of the middle belt has hardly been clear through history." Obviously, this makes the definition of the Middle Belt more tasking than normal.

What is referred to as the Middle Belt is fluid and fluctuates between geography (territorial) and political ideology. In all instances, it is using Christian identity to resist the Muslim hegemony of the Sokoto caliphate. Therefore, the Middle Belt covers both the ideological and geographical dimensions, with particular hints on the Christian identity nuance associated with the history of the concept.

Geographically, Ishaku (2002) stated that the Middle Belt connotes the mid-lands between the Southern and Northern part of the country. Providing further demarcations on what constitutes the "Geographical Middle Belt," Blench (1998) states that the region is the area roughly inscribed by the Hausa-speaking area to the north, and the Yoruba, Edo and Ibo speaking areas to the south.

With this apparent delineation of the Middle Belt subregion in mind, Shilgba (2013) goes on to name the territorial states to include Benue, Nasarawa, Taraba, Adamawa, Niger, Plateau, Southern Kebbi, Kogi, Kwara Niger, Southern Kaduna, Federal Capital Territory (FCT), Southern Gombe, and two minority local government areas of Tafawa Balewa and Bogoro in southern Bauchi state. What this means is that the Middle Belt does not correspond with the current political contraption of the North-central geo-political zone that comprises Benue, Kogi, Nasarawa, Kwara, Plateau and the FCT. Essentially, the contention has always been how 'middle' or central these states are on the geographical map of Nigeria.

From the political and ideological perspective, Ishaku (2002) noted that the Middle Belt connotes an anti-feudal political tendency directed against what has been coined as the Hausa-Fulani oligarchy. It is against this background that Alubo (2006) interprets the Middle Belt to mean "a vehicle for political mobilization and a rallying point in the struggle for identity and political participation" by Christian minorities of Lord Lugard's Northern Nigeria. It is in this connection that it is right "to have posited that the middle belt comprises of people who were non-Hausa speaking, non-Muslim or both" (Sklar, 1963).

The Middle Belt became a category, activating non-Muslim and non-Hausa-Fulani consciousness against Northernization perceived as a ploy to Islamize the North and keeping the ethnic minorities marginalized in the socio-political development of Nigeria.

Obviously, the geographical and political/ideological definitions of the Middle Belt have some contradictions needing resolution. For instance, if viewed from the political and ideological learning, with self-emancipation and determination of non-Muslim and non-Hausa-Fulani ethnic minorities in the North as the hallmark, then the geographical definition negates the non-Muslim and non-Hausa-Fulani minorities in Northern states of Kano, Katsina, Jigawa and Borno.

Though they are not captured by the geographical definition, they share in the ideological quest of rebuffing the caliphate's hegemony. So, how are they to be accounted for? Still, what of indigenous to the subregion who bear Islamic identity and would not compromise it for the political interest of the Middle Belt? What is the stake of such indigenous Muslims in the Middle Belt's struggle that was inspired by Christian missionaries against fellow Muslim folks?

Another point deserving attention is that the ideological or political definition of the Middle Belt excludes those with political sympathy elsewhere who live in the region geographically. For instance, some emirates in Niger State would rather go with the caliphate politically than the Middle Belt where they belong territorially. In the same way, the Yoruba in Kogi, whose ambition will win the sympathy of the South-west, is likely to identify with that region politically instead of the Middle Belt.

These are contentions in the definition of the Middle Belt that need to be resolved. Suffice to align with Lar whom Haruna (2014) has quoted to have said geographically the Middle Belt is distinct from and smaller than the political Middle Belt. The political Middle Belt encompasses all the marginalized minority groups in Northern Nigeria. These are minorities that have historically resisted feudalism, political oppression, injustice, religious discrimination and economic emasculation of the unfavored masses.

The Christian clout associated with the Middle Belt can only be better understood from its origin. The fact is the beginning of its identity predates colonial experience in the subregion. However, the form in which it was manifested in the 1950s and 1960s was activated by angered reactions against the yoke of the colonial masters, in general, and the cultural imperialism of the Muslim Hausa-Fulani in particular.

The activities and legacies of both the colonial masters and Muslim Hausa-Fulani imperialists brought the Middle Belt subregion to what Air Cdre Dan Suleiman (retd) described, quoted by Ibrahim (2013), as a grossly marginalized region with an endangered species on the brink of extinction and cultural annihilation. The colonial masters, after plundering the subregion, showed glaringly the disposition to hand over this script to the newfound bride of the Muslim Hausa-Fulani to continue with the act.

CHAPTER FOUR

Islam and the Idea of the Woman – The Northern Context

This chapter sets out to give a synopsis of not just the idea of the girl-child, but also a brief discourse on women in Islam. I admit that this will not be an easy task due to diverging narratives and conflicting pictures of the woman in Islam. As a matter of fact, different schools of thought in Islam have enjoyed the polemics regarding the topic of the woman. Most subject matters derived from revealed religions are usually controversially understood and addressed.

Providing an insight into this development, Ibuot (2012, p. 130) says that "revelations are impenetrable, even to philosophers. Only oracular experts may be able to make such valuable input." And since I am not an oracular expert, I will, therefore, rely on the opinion of experts; some of whom include Aisha Abd EI Rah-man, and Abd Al-Masih among others. Furthermore, I will align myself with Ahmed (1992) who says that in doing this kind of study, one will have to grapple with cultural ideas or "discourses" about appropriate female roles and conduct. More specifically, with what Leila Ahmed calls "the core discourses of Islam," the Qur'an, (divine revelation), the Sunna (deeds and sayings of the prophet Muhammed), the Hadith (interpretive moral codes based on sayings of the prophet), and other sacred writings.

Having established the resources from which the search for the image of woman in Islam will be eventually drawn, it is key to understand that, in Islam, there are two kinds of women – the perfect woman in paradise and the imperfect woman on earth.

Ibuot (2012) is of the view that the perfect image of the woman is that of a houri, who is in perpetual youthfulness and in a sexually virile condition, especially from the perspective of the man. Drawing from the hadith, Schoeman (2003) reveals that a houri is a most beautiful young woman with a transparent body, her marrow visible, like the interior line of pearls and rubies. She looks like red wine in a white glass. She is white in color and free from routine physical disabilities of an ordinary woman, such as menstruation, menopause, urine and offal discharge, child-bearing and the related pollution. A houri is a girl of tenderness, having large, round breasts, which are not inclined to dangle.

For Ibuot (2012, p. 131), the above description means that "the woman has no worth of her own except to be man's slave and instrument. If that of the perfect woman is slavery, then that of the woman on earth must be hopeless." It is therefore no surprise that bandits and Boko Haram will always treat women and the girl-child as persons who are worthless and, thus, take them as slaves. This interpretation of who a woman is clearly provides the ideological basis that radical Islamic groups will continue to manipulate in order to thwart the future of women and the girl-child.

Using the principle of Takfir, Muslims and non-Muslims, especially women and the girl-child, are taken hostage as slaves of Jihad. Field work in Yobe and Zamfara states shows that in sex slavery, a subtype of slavery, the girl-child in Northern Nigeria suffered the most at the hand of Boko Haram insurgents and bandits. Wood (2006, p.308) defines sexual slavery as, "in some conflicts, sexual violence takes the form of sexual slavery, whereby women are abducted to serve as servants and sexual partners of combatants for extended periods; in others, it takes the form of torture in detention."

As a matter of fact, I align myself with Brownmiller (1975) who has argued that if it were not for this 'accident of biology', rape and sexual violence would not exist. The reason is that sexual violence has nothing to do with sexuality or desire. Rather, it is a violent action in which a male sets out to practice control and dominance over a female. The reason for sexual violence is not natural instinct in a male, but misogyny and war provide males with the perfect context to vent to their contempt for women, so it occurs in conflict situations.

Generally, the Slavery Convention defines slavery as: "(1) ...the status or condition of a person over whom any or all of the powers attaching to the right of ownership are exercised; (2) the slave trade includes all acts involved in the capture, acquisition or disposal of a person with intent to reduce him to slavery; all acts involved in the acquisition of a slave with a view to selling or exchanging him; all acts of disposal by sale or exchange of a slave acquired with a view to being sold or exchanged, and, in general, every act of trade or transport in slaves (1927, art.1)."

It needs to be pointed out that slavery has long been part of the pre-Islamic history of sub-Saharan Africa. Other sources are in agreement that slavery was a mainstay of life in pre-Islamic Arabia and surrounding lands. This shows that the issue of slavery was not limited to sub-Saharan Africa alone. And, when Islam was introduced to the area, the situation remained largely the same. This is likely why Hunwick and Powell

(2002) opine that, as a matter of principle, Islamic law held that the only lawful means to generate slaves was through the capture of non-Muslims who refused to convert during a lawful Jihad.

Enslavement was, in fact, one of five options available to a Muslim captor engaged in a legitimate Jihad. The other four were putting prisoners to death, releasing them without penalty, and/or asking a ransom and demanding the payment of a head tax (jizya). Providing further information on how slavery affects women and the girl-child, Lydon and Hall (2007) say that enslaved women and girls were frequently included in marriage negotiations among the Muslim elite and featured in bride wealth payments. They further reveal that from their cursory examination of marriage contracts and other sources describing civil matters, it would appear that a gender division of property rights prevailed, which included slave ownership.

An example is the case of a woman who was given a young slave girl (ama) by her father at the time of her marriage. Shortly after he died, leaving no records of this particular transaction, the executor of the will claimed the slave. The woman's husband then purchased the slave back for her, but the ownership of the slave was contested once again between the two families after the wife died. It was resolved in a fatwa in favor of the husband's family (Lydon and Hall, 2007).

The girl-child in Northern Nigeria must not be allowed to be a victim of slavery by terrorist groups. Rather, the girl-child must be allowed to gain freedom. Citing ar-Raghib al-Isfahani (ca. 1100) in his Qur'an dictionary, Freamon (2015) says he first defined urr [to be free] as the opposite of 'abd [to be a slave], and then distinguished two forms of urriyya [freedom]: the one referring to the person who is not subject to any authority, and the other to the person who is not dominated by any ugly qualities as greed and the desire for worldly possessions.

In order to illustrate the first form of urriyya, Al-Isfahani referred to the Qur'an's homicide legislation at 2:178-9, which abolished the vendetta and blood feud as a remedy for homicide and substituted an egalitarian approach to capital punishment, ordering that punishment should be meted out according to a regime of rough equality, "the free for the free" (al urr bi-l- urr), "the woman for the woman" and "the slave for the slave" (al 'abd bi-l-'abd). He also pointed to the Qur'anic use of the term t r r, at, for instance, 4:92/94, which means to "liberate" or "free" the slave from his or her shackles. For the second meaning, he proposed an interpretation of mu arrar at 3:35/31 ("where the mother of Moses is said to have dedicated the child in her womb to God mu arraran") as meaning "free from worldly desires."

It is the former use of urr that predominates in the Qur'an, and the great bulk of the Qur'anic discussion of slavery is, therefore, concerned with practical problems involving the treatment of slaves, their relationships to free persons and circumstances governing their emancipation. Even though there is considerable regulation of the relation between the free and the enslaved, there are no verses suggesting that the practice of slavery ought to continue and virtually no discussion of slave trading. Yet, one also looks in vain for an explicit statement mandating the end of the practice. Thus, Boko Haram and bandits are exploiting it and hurting the girl-child in Northern Nigeria.

SECTION TWO

Northern Nigeria: Religious Landscape and Sundry Issues

Violent conflicts have spasmodically erupted in Nigeria, particularly in the Northern part of the country. Providing an analysis of actors in the conflicts, International Crisis Group (2010, p. 3) observes that the violent conflict "has pitted Muslims against Christians and has seen confrontations between different Islamic sects." Northern Nigeria is made up of Muslims, who are arguably the majority, and a substantial Christian minority, both indigenous to the area as well as the product of migration from the Southern region of the country. The fault lines have often been contested between Muslims and Christians, on one hand, and adversarial ideological polemics among sects, on the other.

Regarding the former, Ayoub (2007, p. 43) says that "the relationship between Christians and Muslims globally has been one of "mistrust, misgivings, and misunderstanding." It is argued that several other scholars are concerned largely with relations between the "Christian West" and the "Muslim Arab world". This relationship has enjoyed even more scrutiny largely due to the growing "Islamofascism" wars and conflicts since the September 11, 2001 attacks on the World Trade Center in New York in the United States.

Proving deeper insights into intra-Muslim relations in Nigeria, International Crisis Group (2010) says that debates among Muslims in the region tend to divide those who respect the established religious and secular authorities and their two-century-old Sufi heritage from those who take a "reformist" view. The latter cover a very wide range of opinion, from Salafist-type to anti-Sufism to Iranian-inspired Shiite movements and combine anger at the establishment's corruption with a promise of a more individualistic religious experience.

Typically, some end up being co-opted by both religious and secular authorities, largely due to the latter's control over public resources. But others maintain a hostile or rejectionist stance that, in some isolated cases, turns into violent rejection of public authority. One of such is Boko Haram.

CHAPTER FIVE
Boko Haram

The official name of Boko Haram is Jama'atu Ahl As-Sunna Li-D'awati Wal-Ji-had, which, in Ar-abic, translates to "People Committed to the Propagation of the Prophet's Teachings and Ji-had." The group's intention is to carry out holy war (Jihad) to Islamize Nigeria. The group is named Boko Haram because of its strong aversion to Western education, which the sect members consider to be corrupting Muslims. Meanwhile, Mohammed and Haruna (2010) reveal that the exact date of the establishment of the sect remains unclear, but a majority of analysts, including the security forces in Nigeria, trace it to around 2002-2004.

There is also limited information regarding the sect's first leader who was simply identified as Aminu Tashen-Ilimi. He established the group's base in Kanamma village in Yobe State in approximately 2004. Taiwo and Olugbode (2009) opine that Mohammed Yusuf later emerged as the popular leader of the movement, barely having any Western education and hailing from a poor family background in Jakusko, Yobe State.

According to Thurston (2016), Boko Haram's ideology is often described as comprising two stances: opposition to democracy and rejection of Western-style education. This explains why "Boko Haram" is translated by outsiders to mean Western education is forbidden by Islam. Thurston (2016) further reveals that the movement's spokesmen have sometimes accepted this, but when they do, they insist that the phrase refers not just to schooling but also to social and political ills that allegedly result from the Western domination of Nigerian state and society.

As a matter of fact, the sect's theology and politics encompass more than hatred for Western influence. Its worldview fuses two broader ideas. First, there is a religious exclusivism that opposes all other value systems, including rival interpretations of Islam. This exclusivism demands that Muslims choose between Islam and a set of allegedly anti-Islamic practices: democracy, constitutionalism, alliances with non-Muslims, and

Western-style education.

Second are politics of victimhood. Boko Haram claims that its violence responds to, what it sees, as a decades-long history of persecution against Muslims in Nigeria. Boko Haram sees state crackdowns on the sect as the latest manifestation of such persecution.

Thurston (2016) says that Boko Haram's best-known stance is its rejection of Western-style schooling. Yet the concept of "Boko Haram" encompasses a broader critique of Nigerian society, targeting the perceived fruits of such schools. Boko Haram is not alone in resenting the highly educated Nigerian elites who have failed to deliver prosperity to the majority of Nigerians. Many Nigerians decry widespread corruption in government.

Some Muslims in the North, where classical Qur'anic and Islamic education is a powerful social force, feel ambivalence towards Western-style institutions of learning. On one hand, secondary and tertiary degrees are respected credentials, and Northerners take pride in their region's universities and colleges. On the other hand, some Northern Muslims believe Western-style schools fail to inculcate Islamic values. Boko Haram represents an extreme manifestation of this latter attitude, rejecting compromises, such as "Islamiyya" schools that blend government curricula with religious instruction.

Yusuf objected to the content and effects of Western-style education. Ideas, like Darwinism, he said, contradicted the Quran. Schools led Muslim children to adopt the mannerisms of Jews and Christians. Children of different genders interacted at school, promoting fornication, lesbianism, homosexuality, and other [corruptions] (Yusuf, 2008). Yusuf (2008) further argues that the 'Christianizing' schools of British colonialism are no different than postcolonial government schools, but the prospect of material gain blinded Muslims to the truth "Because of love for this world, many people's hearts have been saturated with love of these schools, until they do not see in them that which contradicts [Islam's] law." Therefore, for Yusuf, the credentials conferred by Western-style schools were useless to genuine Muslims.

However, Mohammed (2013) makes an intriguing observation. According to him, Western education has been classified as part of those things that do not form the fundamentals of worship (ibadat) and, as such, is not important enough for a Muslim to be classified an infidel simply because he accepts Western education. This classification makes it the responsibility of whomever claims that it is prohibited to provide evidence to convince other Muslims. This is because most Muslims consider Western education permissible as long as it does not contradict clear teachings of the Qur'an, Hadiths, and objectives of the Shariah.

The call on Muslims by Boko Haram to reject democracy and to not participate in any electoral process is not the general view of Muslims. For instance, Mustapha

(2014) states that Islam is compatible with democratic politics, and that it is the duty of every Muslim to take part in the electoral system to resist fraud.

CHAPTER SIX

Banditry

Just as many security and social science terms, banditry is a too-fluid term to define. However, it can be said that it covers different variants of outlawry behaviors. On their part, Okoli and Ugwu (2019) say that banditry refers to the incidences of armed robbery or allied violent crimes, such as kidnapping, cattle rustling, and village or market raids. It involves the use of force, or threat to that effect, to intimidate a person or a group of persons in order to rob, rape or kill (Okoli and Okpaleke 2014). Economic or political interests motivate banditry. The former refers to banditries motivated by the imperative of material accumulation, while the latter has to do with those driven by the quest to rob, assault or liquidate a person or group of persons based on political or ideological considerations.

Their modus operandi involves maiming and killing their victims when they least expect. Usually, they mobilize themselves through the forests into the neighborhood riding on fast motorcycles, especially in the nights, shooting at will. Sometimes in the day, once they are sure there is no security presence of the police or military, they unleash terror on the communities. This growing threat is claiming hundreds of victims. Several children have been orphaned and women widowed overnight all while the issue of food security and humanitarian tragedy will further make life unbearable for many Nigerians.

With reference to Northwestern Nigeria, The Humanitarian (2018) avers that the region has a long history of banditry. The first recorded case occurred somewhere between western Hausa land and the Niger border in 1901, when a 12,000-strong camel train, laden with assorted grains, was attacked and 210 merchants killed. Although rural banditry is as old as Nigeria, it has nonetheless incrementally transformed over time from its rudimentary phase to a complex and complicated pattern of criminality (Egwu 2016). This is a pointer to the fact that the phenomenon of banditry predates Nigeria's emergence as a political entity.

In this regard, Jaafar (2018, 2) opines that there were recorded instances of rural banditry in colonial Nigeria "as far back as the 1930s." Providing contextual and sociological explanation of this occurrence, he explains that, in those days, wayfarers and merchants traveling along their local economic roads usually faced the threat and danger of ambush from nondescript bandits. Armed bandits and criminals were known to be targeting goods ferried on the backs of donkeys, camels and ox carts. The bandits on those trade routes would forcefully take those goods and disappear into the bush. However, that is just one dimension of the problem.

In other instances, bandits would raid farming communities and villages with the intent of willful killing and wanton destruction of property. During such raids, the bandits would destroy virtually everything in their path, including valuables, farm produce, etc. This subculture has been in existence even before the coming of colonialists to the territories of Northern Nigeria, and so the modern transformation of rural banditry must be understood against the backdrop of the prevailing national security dialectics in Nigeria. According to Bagu and Smith (2017), gangs of criminals, often youths from farming and herding communities and/or local bandits, would take advantage of growing insecurity, fear and cyclical attacks to loot villages, engage in highway robbery, and rustle cattle for personal gain. Both farming and herding communities suffer from this criminality.

The facts are frightening. For instance, Ademola (2021) reports that while about 1,100 people were murdered in 2018 in the six states of Northwest Nigeria in 2018, over 2,200 were killed in 2019 and 1,600 killed between January and June

2020. He reveals further that about 247,000 people have been displaced, which has led to the production of more than 41,000 refugees. International Crisis Group (2020) disclosed that in Zamfara alone, over 8,000 people were murdered in the last decade, 200,000 displaced internally and others fled to neighboring states. In Sokoto, Mohammed (2020) says that more than 250 people have been killed in about 20 attacks, leaving the Sultan of Sokoto, Muhammadu Sa'ad Abubakar 111, to lament that bandits now move freely in the North from house to house wielding AK47s, as the region has become the worst place to live in Nigeria (Onyebuchi, 2020).

Another source, West African Network for Peacebuilding (WANEP 2020) says that a total of 6,319 deaths, including women and children between June 2011 and May 2019, happened in the State. Additionally, an estimated 4,983 women were widowed, 25,050 children orphaned, and 190,340 others internally displaced between June 2011 and May 2019 in Zamfara State. In Katsina State, one of the states in the Northwestern geopolitical zone, over 2,000 people have been killed, 500 communities destroyed and over 33,000 people displaced.

This goes to show that the Northwestern region of Northern Nigeria has been worst hit by banditry. Buttressing this point, International Crisis Group (2020) says that Nigeria's Northwest is suffering deadly conflict involving many armed organizations, including herder-allied groups, vigilantes, criminal gangs and jihadists. The violence has killed over 8,000 people since 2011 and displaced over 200,000, some into neighboring Niger. Despite several security operations and dialogue efforts, a durable peace remains elusive.

Providing a detailed description of the Northwest zone, Abdullahi (2019) explains that it is one of the largest geopolitical zones in Nigeria in terms of landmass and population. The zone covers 192,689 km - equivalent to 83,415 square meters of land - with a combined population of about 40 million of Nigeria's 200 million people (NBS, 2017). Hausa and Fulani ethnic groups are predominant in the Northwest with minority groups across the geopolitical zone. The zone is comprised of seven states: Sokoto, Zamfara, Kebbi, Katsina, Kaduna, Kano, and Jigawa.

CHAPTER SEVEN

Typology of Banditry

Typological Index

Social vs. political vs. economic	Intent or motive
Rural vs. urban	Location
Mercenary vs. autonomous	Agency and autonomy
Organized vs. petty	Form and formation
Roving vs. stationary	Operational mode
Frontier vs. countryside	Location
Maritime vs. coastal vs. mainland	Location

SOURCE: Okoli and Ugwu (2019)

As shown in the Typological Index, banditry can be classified on its underlying intent or motive. In this regard, one can talk of 'social banditry' that is generally motivated by the intent to protest social inequality and redistribute wealth within a locality. Likewise, one could speak of other forms of banditry that are principally motivated by political or economic reasons. When location of occurrence is the underlying index, one can speak in terms of rural versus urban or frontier versus countryside banditry, as the case may be. Similarly, banditry can be mercenary or autonomous, depending on how the actor of agency is played out.

Mercenary banditry is perpetuated by auxiliaries or mercenaries working for a principal in a sort of principal-agent relationship, while autonomous bandits are self-motivated and personally commissioned. Organized banditry thrives on a network of syndicated and coordinated actors while petty banditry is perpetrated by individual or group actors that are not as organized. Roving bandits are more or less mobile or itinerant while stationary bandits are settled or sedentary. Lastly, maritime banditry refers to offshore robbery (piracy) as compared to those that occur on the coast or mainland.

CHAPTER EIGHT

Drivers of Banditry

A significant part of the Northwest zone is dry yet fertile land, agrarian for farming and livestock development. In spite of the potential of the Northwest, since the return of democracy, it has experienced devastating rural banditry, which claims thousands of lives and property. This began as localized disputes between headers and farmers over access to land and water resources. However, poor handling of the rural banditry has significantly contributed to its transformation into a deadly conflict posing a major threat to national and regional security and integration.

Abduallahi (2019) says the pattern and intensity of rural banditry in the Northwest are connected to socio-economic, environmental, and political forces which shape the development of the geopolitical zone. The first is what could be described as environmental forces caused partly by climatic conditions and changes the subregion is faced with. For instance, the Northwest has been affected by drought, food insecurity, flooding and shrinking of rivers due to changes in climatic conditions. These changes influenced herders' and farmers' movement from one area to another, in most cases beyond the zone in search of water resources and grazing land. Where this movement coincides with the harvesting period, it becomes a source of conflicts between farmers and herders with devastating effects on the agricultural and livestock development of the Northwest.

Farmers and herders who lost their farmlands and products or cattle resort to rural banditry as a means of survival. Corroborating this view, Malumfashi and Kaina (2021) citing their interview with some of the bandits, report that the bandits claim that they – and others like them – have turned to hostage-taking and other crimes because they have little choice to survive. The bandits who are mostly ethnic Fulani are traditionally nomadic herders who have seen public grazing lands shrink and their cattle and sheep stolen by soldiers and rustlers. They said various governments have neglected and even harassed them, failing to protect their way of life. The herders further lament that this country is blessed with oil and other natural resources, but that bounty doesn't filter down.

Added to the growing tension over resources between farmers and herders is a rivalry between self-help groups, mostly the Hausa, who are deployed by local communities to curtail the insurgency and the herders, predominantly the Fulani, who are accused of rural banditry across Nigeria. The rivalry, particularly in Zamfara and Katsina states, was a product of long-time incessant and indiscriminate handling of grievances between the two ethnic groups by the local traditional rulers. Each group accused leadership of maltreatment and outright indiscrimination on matters involving land and cattle ownership. This was further aggravated by hate speeches, name-calling, and the failure of the state to handle these problems effectively. Thus, as the rivalry intensified, both groups resorted to sexual assault of women and female children and burning of local food reserves in villages.

The rivalry increased tribal tension, thereby raising credibility questions of traditional institutions and eventually led to the loss of lives and properties from the two groups. According to Egbejule (2018), farmer and herder conflicts arising from loss of farms and/or cattle as well as intertribal rivalry turned to banditry and resorted to indiscriminate kidnapping, murder and abducting women as well as forcing them into sex slavery. Closely connected to the foregoing is the gradual disappearance of grazing land and routes caused by the indiscriminate allocation of lands and poor implementation of urban and regional development plans across the Northwest.

In the past, colonial and post-colonial governments across Nigeria have made deliberate institutional and livestock development policies for acquisition and maintenance of grazing lands and routes. Regrettably, the discovery of oil and the subsequent neglect of the agricultural sector contributed to the gradual confiscation and handing over of grazing lands and cattle routes for urban and land development programs. State governors who are constitutionally responsible for land allocation and development blatantly abused and misused such powers for political benefits.

According to Abdullahi (2019), some state governors moved around with land titles and certificates as a political tool to generate support from elites and the electorates. Political patronage, tribute and prebendalism guide the allocation of lands and development in most parts of the Northwest. Abdullahi (2019) further explains that empirical evidence shows that some of these lands located in places, such as Birnin-Gwari Kaduna, Tureta in Sokoto and Birnin-Magaji in Zamfara State, were used for the construction of farmhouses and filling stations.

While some of these urban development programs are desirable, many others were of no relevance to rural development as they only intensified agricultural capitalism for easy access to agricultural facilities and loans from financial institutions. For Egwu (2016), the dynamics associated with the disappearance of grazing lands and routes altered agrarian relations and further complicated social relations among occupational groups across Nigeria. This forced Fulani herders, farmers and other occupational groups to employ banditry tactics to compete for scarce land and water resources, which sometimes degenerated into rural banditry and other forms of domestic insurgencies in Nigeria.

Another factor that is sustaining rural banditry is elite conspiracy influenced by the quest for primitive accumulation of power and wealth. For example, political elites across parties, who lost the election and are dissatisfied with the state leadership, support and conspire bandit groups to discredit political leadership and erode its legitimacy in the eyes of the electorates. This probably explains why Governor Bello Mohammed Matawalle of Zamfara State has consistently argued that some political gladiators in the state are responsible for the conflict. This position was confirmed at the Focal Group Discussion in Talata Mafara and Zurmi towns of Zamfara State.

Apart from political elites, some traditional rulers are also involved in aiding and abetting rural banditry in the Northwest and other parts of Northern Nigeria. For example, participants at a focal group discussion in Gwako community of Gwagwalada Area Council in the Federal Capital Territory (FCT), Abuja reveal that a chief in the Anagada community was dethroned because of his involvement in banditry activities. Abdullahi (2019) says that empirical evidence shows that some traditional rulers provide safety to bandit groups to carry out their illicit operations. They are accused of blatantly refusing to take action against rural bandits' activities in their communities. It is no longer something new that rural bandits enjoyed unprecedented immunity from traditional rulers and were seen walking freely with dangerous weapons around local markets.

It was gathered at a focal group discussion that bandits have formed the habit of attacking innocent people, imposing toll collection and demanding ransom from traders and buyers on local market days in Shinkafi, Birnin Magaji and other local communities in Zamfara State. In some cases, traditional rulers appoint their agents to negotiate terms and conditions of collaboration with the bandits on their behalf. In this regard, cases of banditry brought before the traditional rulers were either discharged without any serious interrogation or backfired on the communities.

It is intriguing that participants at a focal group discussion in Tsanni of Katsina State as well as Shinkafi of Zamfara State did not mind the seeming dangerous consequence, accusing public officials in state security institutions of also becoming part of the conspiracy through outright misappropriation of funds meant for the welfare of security personnel and supply of arms to fight banditry in the Northwest. This is evident in the series of alleged cases of misappropriation and outright embezzlement of funds meant for military and police operations across Nigeria. This was further compounded by the failure of the Nigerian police and military leadership to monitor their operations closely in areas devastated by rural banditry.

Abdullahi (2019) explains that most senior military officers in charge of field operations hardly go to the field to have an on-the-spot idea on welfare, operational and technical challenges affecting their personnel. Instead, they were mostly lodged in hotels and government guest houses at the instance of the state. This idea of using hotels and guest houses as control centers of the army affects command, control, and operations of the war against banditry in the Northwest.

It also denies the military hierarchy the opportunity to have transparent and credible intelligence that would improve military operations in the affected areas. Closely connected to the foregoing is a poor inter-agency collaboration between the major segments of the army, on one hand, and other security agencies, such as the Nigerian Police and Department of State Services (DSS), on the other. There were reported cases of lack of information sharing and poor coordination between the land army and air force in most areas affected by rural banditry in Nigeria.

This poor handling of the conflict coupled with the terrible working conditions under which officers and men prosecute the war has raised capacity and credibility questions on the sincerity of political leadership in dealing with the conflict. Added to elite conspiracy was the involvement of families and relations of victims of banditry in providing information to bandits in exchange for monetary incentives. Many families were confirmed to serve as an errand to bandit groups by providing them with information on the location, time, and whereabouts of their victims. This indicates the degeneration of moral, cultural, and ethical values of brotherhood and communitarian tradition of African societies. It has created suspicions among families with negative consequences on state-society relations in the continent.

Apart from the elite conspiracy, state and non-state institutions have also contributed to the rise of rural banditry in the Northwest. One such institutions is the media in Nigeria, which has become polarized and biased in their reporting and coverage of rural banditry in the subregion. The conflict is underreported, and little attention is given to it in popular public discourse. Additionally, hate speeches, name calling and the use of offensive language, particularly on social media platforms by politicians and private media owners further complicate public order and the problem of rural banditry (Abdullahi, 2019).

Indeed, the Nigerian media has become part of the conspiracy, escalating farmer-herder conflicts and other forms of domestic insurgency in the country. It is in this regard that Ibrahim (2016) argues that the narratives of rural banditry by the media and in popular discourse are becoming part of the drivers for expanding conflicts in Nigeria. The biased nature of the Nigerian media reports on rural banditry could be seen as a grand design meant to create public disorder instead of serving as a medium of providing a solution to the problem of banditry in the country.

CHAPTER NINE

Boko Haram and Bandits – Point of Convergence and Divergence

After the abduction of the schoolboys at the Government Science Secondary School in Kankara of Katsina State, Anyadike (2021) said that the abductors, in a video message, spoke of their link with Boko Haram, a claim endorsed by the jihadist group. However, this claim is taken with mixed feelings across pundits and residents of the affected areas. For instance, while some participants agree that the bandits have strong ties with Boko Haram, others disputed the view, insisting that bandits are identifying with Boko Haram in order to launder their image. This too, is doubtful. It is particularly so because Malumfashi and Kaina (2021) aver that the bandits wield influence across the French-speaking countries of Mali, Senegal, Burkina Faso, Cameroon and Central African Republic. This is indicative that the bandits ordinarily will have no reason to launder their image.

Ideologically, Boko Haram is incurably opposed to Western education and everything associated with it. This, therefore, makes it understandable why schools will come under the attack of the group. In a related development, the Guardian newspaper (2021) laments the full-scalc onslaught on education in Nigeria by Islamist extremists. The newspaper further reveals that Boko Haram wars against education, as bandits are mass kidnapping children in school and religious violence against Christian mission school owners in Ilorin over hijab controversy, is assuming a very dangerous dimension. For the Northern Region of Nigeria that grapples with lack of education for the girl-child, this is not the best of times, and these events will have deeper rooted effects than can be imagined at the moment.

That notwithstanding, Boko Haram's vexation and the stated reason for attack on schools is the refusal of the Nigerian state to fund Tsangaya in the same manner as Western style schools. Validating this view, Mahmood (2017) argues that public threats to schools emerged ahead of a campaign in which classrooms were burnt down in retaliation for the supposed mistreatment of almajiri students and teachers (part of the traditional Tsangaya Islamic schooling system). For example, in a January 26, 2012 message, Shekau complained about this alleged mistreatment and threatened to launch attacks. Mark (2012) reports that at around the same time, Qaqa, the spokesman of Boko Haram, warned that the sect would begin bombing private schools.

This suggests that the campaign began via public warnings rooted in a specific grievance linked to perceptions of mistreatment before morphing into outright violence. Interestingly, the campaign to burn down schools was initially designed to avoid civilian casualties before the attacks intensified to include students as victims. Explaining this approach, Idris quotes Qaqa as saying that "we attacked the schools at night because we don't want to kill pupils ... we would attack the public school in daylight if any Tsangaya school is attacked again." This clearly reveals the pathway to escalation.

For Boko Haram, abduction is for the sole purpose of conversion to their own style of Islamic faith. It means that violent style proselytization is their motivating factor. An example that puts this argument into context is the abduction of 110 schoolgirls at Government Girls' Science and Technical College, Dapchi, located in Yunusari Local Government of Yobe State at about 5:30 pm on February 19, 2018. Different sources suggest that the government of the Federal Republic of Nigeria, using an under-the-table arrangement via some protégé abroad, paid for the ransom of the girls, which led to their release.

Yet, a Christian girl named Leah Sharibu was not released because she refused to convert to Islam. On January 1, 2019 the Guardian newspaper named her its 2018 'Person of the Year,' aptly describing her as "a goddess of resistance" (Guardian Newspaper, 2021). Put in another way, Uchegbu (2021, p. 16) says that "she was offered conversion to the religion of her abductors as bait for freedom".

In a related development, Barnabas Aid (2021) reports that another Christian, Pastor Bulus Yakuru, was abducted in Borno State on Christmas Eve. The militants snatched the pastor during a raid on the predominantly Christian village of Pemi, about 20 kilometers from Chibok, in which 11 people were killed on 24th of December in 2016. The gunmen went on to murder five Christians abducted in the region as a so-called 'Christmas present.'

Attacks on churches and the killing of Christians by Boko Haram is another area of study that deserves special attention from scholars. The record of the churches and number of Christians killed by the group is simply unavailable due to poor documentation and the manner in which these attacks occur. However, worthy of mention is the attack on St. Theresa's Catholic, Madala, located on the fringes of Niger state and Abuja, during which scores of worshippers were killed and eventually buried as martyrs.

Zakariya Musa, head of media for Ekklesiyar Yan'uwa a Nigeria (EYN, the Church of the Brethren in Nigeria) says Garkida, a town in the Gombi Local Government Area of Adamawa State in Northeast Nigeria, was attacked. During the attack, several churches, including EYN Ghung, EYN Sangere, and Living Faith Church Garkida were burnt. The Living Faith Church was rebuilt after the attack of February 21, 2016 when four churches were destroyed in a similar attack. Three more churches and many houses were destroyed at Tashan Alade, Kirbitu, and Debiro towns. The destroyed churches include those that were destroyed in 2014, which were later rebuilt by the Borno State Government. The renewed attacks are coming on an almost daily basis in different ways, resulting in killings, kidnapping, destruction of properties and the like (Church of the Brethren, 2020).

Meanwhile, it is important to point out that the attacks on churches and killing of Christians is theologically justified by Boko Haram in its association of the Christian faith with Western colonialism. It is like saying being a non-Muslim is bad but being a Christian, which is inseparable from Western colonialism, makes one's case double tragedy. On other hand, Muslims who are not proponents of the sect's ideology or deemed to be participating in democratic system are termed as apostates. In the context of takfir, they are made to be subject to attacks. Consequently, and like Christians, scores of Muslims are killed and many Mosques destroyed.

There are so many of such examples to cite, but that is not the focus of this discourse. However, suffice to give a few examples. Aljazeera (2020) says that bandits killed five worshippers and killed 18 others, including the Imam during Friday congregational prayers in Dutsen Gari village of Maru Local Government of Zamfara State.

For bandits, there is not strong evidence or demonstrable argument that their abduction is for faith-based reasons. Though, a focal group discussion in Ankwa, near Kachia town of Kachia Local Government Area of Kaduna State seems to suggest that a Catholic priest in the area was abducted by bandits and killed because of his Christian faith. However, some participants disagreed with this view and said the priest was just a victim of what they called 'political crime.' It was further revealed that the victim was a fearless preacher, who spoke severely against the ills of the government, especially its inability to provide good governance. Preliminary intelligence gathered from the village suggests that some of the bandits operate hand-in-hand with politicians.

Due to this unholy alliance, politicians are likely to use the bandits against their perceived or real enemies. Intriguingly, it can be best resolved that the case of this priest's death is due to premeditated intention of his 'enemies' and the economic opportunity that his abduction would bring to the bandits. The likely assumption is that abducting him would make the Catholic Church, which is considered rich, pay huge sums for his ransom, after which he will be eliminated as wished by his adversaries who contracted them. If this is anything to go by then, economic motivation, rather than faith, was the dominant force in his abduction and eventual execution.

A focal group discussion in Kaura-Namoda in Zamfara State with staff of the Federal Polytechnic, a school where bandits abducted 3 staff and killed one, reveals that, more than ever, the issue of illegal mining of gold and other related mineral resources is responsible. It was argued that bandits collude with foreign interest groups, who supply them with sophisticated guns to displace the local population so illegal mining can take place undisturbed. Participants were unanimous in asserting that the relationship between banditry and illegal mining can be likened to two sides of a coin. Both are inseparable. There was a consensus that banditry and mining is a huge economic capital that the captains are doing everything possible to sustain.

Though illegal mining is prohibited, no one has thus far been prosecuted and jailed for doing it. This goes to buttress the accusation that crime and criminality thrive in Nigeria because of the lack of effective law enforcement. In Illela, a local government in Sokoto that shares a border with the Republic of Niger, participants at a focal group discussion disclosed that the ungoverned space of Nigeria makes it nearly impossible to stop the influx of dangerous weapons and movement of illegal materials in and out of the country.

A similar position was canvased in Kukawah town of Borno State. Participants at a focal discussion group were unequivocal that the ungoverned spaces of Nigeria are now the safe haven for Boko Haram. This goes to show that both bandits and members of Boko Haram are exploiting the inability of the Nigerian state to govern its spaces to commit heinous crimes, wreaking havoc on the citizens, especially the girl-child and women, in general.

A key informant reveals that, because Nigerian spaces are not governed, Boko Haram has made Sambisa Forest its habitable abode. Similarly, bandits have made the Rugu forest their home. In these forests, the insurgents have power generating sets, a thriving prostitution market as well as peddlers of hard drugs.

Rugu is a thick forest stretching from Birnin Gwari in Kaduna State, passing through Katsina State and ending in the present Zamfara State, approximately 220 kilometers in length. Its name is traced to one pronounced hunter, said by Sunday Trust (2012) that Rugu is a popular name of a community leader in Katsina State. Rugu was a fearless and courageous warrior who excelled in hunting and combat during his reign. He was praised by his people as 'Rugu Kan Kura Kowa ya taba ka zai kwana lahira', which literally means 'Rugu, a hyena's head, whoever faces you will die'.

The prominent warrior and his people lived in a forest in the present Safana Local Government Area of Katsina State. Because of Rugu's popularity, the forest, which he occupied with his people, was named after him, is now called Dajin Rugu. It went from being a haven to wild animals, to a camp for Fulani cattle rearers, thieves and armed robbers. However, even the Fulani are currently migrating from Rugu with their herds because of lack of water and grass for their animals.

This is not to mean that the Fulani are no longer in the forest. In fact, the Fulani currently residing in Dajin Rugu are not stationed in one place, instead are scattered across the forest. Every household occupies its own settlement, popularly known as "Mashekari" in Hausa. In these settlements, there is no form of government presence in any form. It is simply a lawless land, meant for lawless persons as events are recently proving to be.

According to Sunday Trust (2012), the forest is blessed with dams and rocks as well. Kurgyel, Mai-Magurzai, Kangurtsa, Yi-Naka, Tsamre Kirya and Zobe, were among the popular rivers and dams in Rugu Forest. Kauni, Rugu and Dagwarwa are the famous rocks that beautify Dajin Rugu. This is in addition to various hills and smaller rocks situated at different locations within the forest. Though many wild animals have left the forest, people from all nooks and crannies do still visit Kauni rock for spiritual purposes.

The Sambisa Forest, also known as Sambisa Game Reserve, is located between Longitude 13°30' and 14°00' East and Latitude 11°00' and 11° 30' North, about 70 kilometers south of Maiduguri in Borno State and is located 14 kilometers off Kawuri village along Maiduguri-Bama Road. The reserve is located in an area of low human population density, cutting across three local government areas of the State, namely Konduga, Gwoza and Bama. The major tribes are Kanuri, Fulani, Gamargu and Gwoza whose occupations are farming and livestock rearing. The reserve covers an area of 518 square kilometers on a fairly flat land drained by three seasonal flowing streams (Kwada, Sambisa and Yuwe), which are tributaries of River Yedzeram (Akosim, et al, 2015).

Corroborating the aforementioned, Olaniyan (2018) says that covering about 518 square kilometers of landscape on a flatland drained by the Ngadda and Yedseram Rivers, Sambisa's lush greenery could rightfully be called a pearl in the semi-desert environment that characterizes most parts of the upper region of Northern Nigeria. Explaining further, he reveals that Sambisa was a long-time home to a variety of wild animals, such as bush elephants, leopards, lions, hyenas, baboons, monkeys of various species and gazelle, as well as about 62 different species of birds. It was also rich in flora, such as acacia, baobab, rubber, tamarind, terminalia and date palm, to mention a few.

As late as the 1970s, Sambisa attracted tourists for safaris. Today, however, the story has changed. The once thriving game reserve is dead. The animals are gone. What remains in abundance in the green landscape is a battalion of Nigerian troops battling a motley band of brutal terrorists that specialize in killings, bombings, beheadings, and the abduction of women and girls for sex slavery.

According to Aju and Aju (2018), Boko Haram insurgents captured and took hold of Sambisa Forest Reserve in 2013. All the surrounding villages to the reserve were also attacked and taken over. In order to seize full control of the forest, the insurgents began a tactical attack on all routes leading to it and, by doing so, made it difficult for any other force to penetrate them.

Providing a historical perspective to this discourse, Abert (2017) says that during the Cold War, rebel movements were sponsored from outside Africa to fight their governments. But after the end of the Cold War in the late 1980s, the rebels had to seek ways of generating the needed financial resources for fighting battles.

Many of them turned to illegal exploitation of forest resources as well as extortionate terrorism, such as kidnapping and hostage-taking, similar to those carried out by bandits. From the foregoing, it is safe to say that the history of Sambisa Forest and others is a history of a nation that does not know what to do with its forests, leaving them as ungoverned spaces.

Though the concept of ungoverned spaces is highly contested and some scholars even question its real existence, the description of Rugu, Sambisa and other forests in Nigeria point to the reality of unrestricted space. Typical of a catch-all term, the description of ungoverned spaces is not definitive.

The Office of US Department of Defense (2007) classifies it as a place where the state or central government is unable or unwilling to extend control, effectively govern, or influence the local population, and where a provincial, local, tribal, or autonomous government does not fully or effectively govern, due to inadequate governance capacity, insufficient political will, gaps in legitimacy, the presence of conflict, or restrictive norms of behavior. Ungoverned areas should be assumed to include under-governed, ill-governed, contested and exploitable areas, which include land, air-space and even cyberspace.

Focal group discussion in the Kagara area of Niger State reveals that bandits have helicopters bringing them food and other supplies, including illicit drugs and arms. This claim corroborates a similar view expressed in Agatu and Ayilamo axis of Logo Local area; all in Benue State. In Borno, different communities have also complained of the same situation. This, therefore, makes one wonder about the level of complicity on the part of Nigerian air space agencies allowing flights that are aiding and abetting crime and criminality.

This emphasizes the different threats posed by ungoverned spaces. They harbor terrorism associated with global jihadism, provide bases for non-jihadi terrorism and criminal networks, and are areas of humanitarian crisis proven to be the most threatening. It is also the case that a humanitarian crisis could precipitate a process that moves beyond a population criticizing the ineffectiveness of the present state to one that seeks to supplant the leadership, as Boko Haram is attempting.

Taylor (2016) argues that 'ungoverned' implies powerful overtones of threat, instability and insecurity, as well as the sense that an ungoverned space is something the affected territory and international state system should avoid at virtually any cost.

The Lake Chad Commission (2019) observes that in many places around the Lake Chad region, the State is effectively absent or maintains very weak presence, reinforcing people's lack of trust in government. The limited infrastructure limits the extent to which the government's presence is felt, particularly in the borderlands and islands in and around the Lake. The lack of and limited access to basic service provisions has increased the perception of marginalization and neglect, created pockets of fragility, led to the breakdown of the social contract, and left people in some areas isolated and vulnerable to recruitment by violent groups.

According to the UNDP (2018), there is a need to re-establish and rebuild public services to make them more functional and easily available to communities. Violent extremist groups seek to fill this gap by offering financial incentives and income-generating opportunities to potential recruits. Islamic State's West African Province (ISWAP) and Boko Haram control trade, impose taxes and facilitate agricultural and livelihoods to increase

its support in exchange for a range of services to secure its position. According to Samuel (2019), economic viability and control is as important to extremist groups' resilience as military tactics or ideology.

The root causes of the deteriorating security situation in the Lake Chad Basin can also be found in divisive reforms and weak governance in the region, coupled with rising inequality and dismay at corruption among the ruling elite (Sauer, 2019). In fact, UNDP (2018) says that on various occasions, corrupt practices have been reported at border crossings, and security personnel blamed for involvement in drug trafficking.

In addition, persistent human rights violations by governments and armed groups have contributed to the deepening of mistrust and created an environment in which joining non-state actors, including Boko Haram and ISWAP, can seem attractive. The intensifying religious fundamentalism and rise of armed militancy is taking place in the context of a power vacuum and perceived lack of state legitimacy. By occupying dozens of Lake Chad island villages, ISWAP has set up state-like structures in North-east Nigeria.

One of the defining characteristics of ungoverned spaces is lack or near lack of state authority. In order to fill this gap, non-state actors form their own government and take control of such territories. Nizzero (2018) says that the common assumption is that the lack of a state authority equates to anarchy. However, it can be argued that there is evidence suggesting the existence of a social order even in areas where armed groups are present. It is also important to point out that the armed groups are not responsible for the existence of the ungoverned spaces, rather, they are simply exploiting them, which is why Taylor (2016) explains that though ungoverned spaces can pose a significant security threat, terrorist groups are seldom, if ever, responsible for the creation of these spaces.

As underlined by Phillips (2015,), there is a surprising lacuna regarding what constitutes a terrorist group, per se. In order to unbundle the concept of terrorist groups, Nizzero (2018) distinguishes between two types of approaches; exclusive and inclusive. The first approach makes a key distinction between groups that hold a territory and groups that do not, defining only the latter as "terrorist." The second approach, on the other hand, argues that territory-holding groups using terrorism have a great deal in common with terrorist groups that do not.

Thus, these groups, regardless of their territorial control, are engaging in a terrorist acts, which are characterized by three main elements: (i) intentional violence, (ii) the aim to spread fear in a wider audience; and (iii) have political motivation (Schmid 2004). The 9/11 Commission (2014) reports that to find sanctuary, terrorist organizations have fled to some of the least governed, most lawless places in the world, areas that combine rugged terrain, weak government, room to hide or receive supplies, and low population density with a town or city near enough to allow necessary interaction with the outside world.

Both Boko Haram and bandits have the following in common: The use of motor cycles to coordinate attacks; a demonstration of mastery of the ungoverned spaces, navigating uncommon routes in order to undermine security intelligence; taxing local communities and threatening that failure to comply will result in attacks; raiding and maiming, especially at night; subjugation of victims to torture; attacks on schools in general and, in recent times, girl schools are of particular interest.

Both Boko Haram and bandits share the same grievance of neglect and marginalization against the Nigerian State. For Boko Haram, Slachmuilder (2017) specifies the following characteristics:

1. Ideology, beliefs and values, including "us vs. them" worldviews, justification of violence and views of certain cultures or nation states as threatening.
2. Psychological factors, such as a desire for purpose or adventure and concerns for individual or group security, all of which may be exacerbated by issues,

such as previous trauma, post-traumatic stress disorder (PTSD), or mental illness.

3. Political grievances related to human rights abuses, limited political and civil liberties, corruption, and foreign occupation.
4. Economic factors, like unemployment, relative poverty, and financial incentives for membership.
5. Sociological motivators, such as alienation, struggling cultural adaptation, marginalization, discrimination and kinship ties.

For Boko Haram, Human Rights (2020) says that the group has conducted numerous attacks on government and civilian targets, resulting in thousands of deaths and injuries, widespread destruction, the internal displacement of more than two million persons and external displacement of more than an estimated 300,000 Nigerian refugees to neighboring countries.

Instructively, Human Rights (2020) further reveals that Boko Haram continued to deploy indiscriminate person-borne improvised explosive device (PIED) attacks targeting local civilian populations with women and children forced to carry out many of the attacks. According to a 2017 study by UNICEF, children, forced by Boko Haram, carried out nearly one in five PIED attacks. More than two-thirds of these children are girls.

CHAPTER TEN

Boko Haram and Bandits – The Challenge of Wrong Framing and its Implication on National Security

According to Gudaku (2021), framing of any form of insecurity is key to interrogating, dissecting and applying the right remedies. However, he laments that this is missing in the gamut of security analysis in Nigeria, particularly as it pertains to Boko Haram, bandits and herdsmen. He explains further that the activities referred to as banditry are no different from what Boko Haram has been doing. Yet, the wrong framing has made stakeholders approach the issue of bandits differently than Boko Haram. Gudaku (2021) insists that this is an indicator and pointer to the fact that wrong framing veils whatever reality that is to be examined.

On the contrary, the right framing will exhume hidden silhouettes that might be because framing is the construction of social reality. It is against this background that Hallahan (1999) reveals that framing is a critical activity in the construction of social reality because it helps shape the perspectives through which people see the world. This, therefore, underscores framing as a paradigm for strategic action. It is in light of this that some scholars argue that the framing of Boko Haram, bandits and herdsmen is deliberate and skewed with the intent of concealing the overriding dangers that portend to the body polity.

Hollahan (1999) contends that framing involves processes of inclusion and exclusion as well as emphasis. Entman (1993) summarizes the essence of framing processes, stating that framing essentially involves selection and salience. He explains further that to frame is to select some aspects of perceived reality and make them more salient in the communicating text in such a way as to promote a particular problem definition, causal interpretation, moral evaluation and/or treatment recommendation for the item described. Frames (1) define problems by determining what a causal agent is doing and the costs and benefits, usually measured in terms of cultural values; (2) diagnose causes by identifying the forces creating the problem; (3) make moral judgments by evaluating causal agents and their effects; and (4) suggest remedies by offering and justifying treatments for the problem along with predictions on their likely effects.

According to Reese, framing is an "organizing principle that is socially shared and persistent over time, that works symbolically to meaningfully structure the social world" (2001, p. 11). Hollahan (1999) reveals that a frame limits or defines the message's meaning by shaping the inferences that individuals make about the message. Frames reflect judgments made by message creators or framers and can represent alternative balancing of information, such as spinning information in either a positive or negative light, or valence framing.

Other frames involve the simple, alternative phrasing of terms (semantic framing). The most complex form of framing is storytelling (story framing), which involves selecting key themes or ideas that are the focus of the message and incorporating a variety of storytelling or narrative techniques that support that theme. Providing further clarification, Pinto (2014) says that framing refers to any situation whereby an actor tries to convince a given audience (or a target group) to participate in/mobilize for and/or believe in a certain idea. This shows that security threats are socially constructed. This process, described by Rychnovska (2012), is called securitization.

Pinto (2014) points out that Copenhagen and its 'ideology of hope' originally theorizes what security is by looking at what it does. This would surmise that Boko Haram, herdsmen and bandits are all involved in doing unprovoked and unwarranted harm. It also means that Waever (1995) is correct in stating that framing is a speech act with presumably established social connotations. Thus, the concept of social constructionism has paved the way for the construct of framing (Scheufele, 2000).

Frames can be understood as 'conceptual structures or sets of beliefs that organize political thought, policies, and discourse' (Van Dijk, 2001: 360). Since 'to frame is to select some aspects of a perceived reality and make them more salient' (Entman 1993: 53), frames are supposed to schematically interpret the 'world out there' through language (Goffman, 1974:21). Similarly, to the contextual reading of securitization, which emphasizes the intersubjective nature of securitization, framing is defined as 'an active, processual phenomenon that implies agency and contention at the level of reality construction' (Benford–Snow, 2000: 614). Inter alia, framing theory deals with the questions of how collective meaning is created through discursive interactions and how it is affected by shared assumptions. This understanding of framing as a specific type of discursive practice comes close to the logic of securitization.

Chinedu et al (2018) are of the view that the theory of securitization is utilized in the field of international relations and security studies. This theory was propounded by the societal security theorists Wæver, Buzan and Wilde (1998) from Copenhagen School (CS) but became popular among the constructivist studies (Theiler, 2010). The term securitization as was coined by Wæver (1995) is the process by which state actors transform subjects into matters of security that enables extraordinary measures to be taken in matters of security.

According to Messina (2014), securitization is a process by which ostensibly non-security issues are transformed into urgent security concerns, which are therefore portrayed as existential threats to a referent object by a securitizing actor who thereby generates endorsement of emergency measures beyond rules that would otherwise bind. It has also been conceptualized as process-oriented actions towards security threats, which is contrary to materialist approaches of classical security studies. Unlike the classical approaches to security that focus on the material dispositions of threats (like the use of power, military capabilities and polarity), securitization emphasizes how an actor can transform a certain issue into a matter of security (threat) in order to allow for the use of extraordinary measures to address it.

Though most securitized issues do not pose an essential threat to objective survival of a state, there is the need to proactively construct a pending security threat to an existential problem. Wæver et al (1998) characterize an existential threat as one that requires immediate solution and if not tackled, makes everything else irrelevant as we may not have the opportunity to deal with the consequences. The framework for securitization allows for a threat to be probable and protracted with the potential to endanger the existence of the nation.

According to the securitization theorists, when a subject is successfully securitized, a higher degree of attention and resources are devoted to it despite the existence of other subjects posing more threat but are unsuccessfully securitized. For instance, terrorism has been successfully securitized and receives more attention than malaria, which kills more people. Therefore, securitization of a subject plays a key role in attracting attention to an existential problem. The success of a securitization process depends on who securitizes (securitizing actor), what issues are securitized (threats), for whom (referent object), the audience (people), the reason for securitization, the conditions of securitization and the results of the securitization acts (Wæver and Wilde, 1998).

The securitizing actor or agent makes the securitizing move or statement. The move follows the establishment of an existential threat, an object or ideal that has been identified as being potentially harmful if left unchecked. A referent object or ideal is that which is being threatened and requires protection. The audience is the target of the securitization act that needs to be persuaded to accept the issue as a security threat, which, if successful, is achieved regardless of whether the subject matter being securitized is a real threat or not. If a subject is successfully securitized, then it is possible to legitimize extraordinary means to solve a perceived problem, which could include declaring a state of emergency.

According to Wæver and Wilde (1998), securitization can be applied mainly on five sectors: military, political, economic, society and environment. However, securitization could be applied equally in many other sectors and further extended to unwanted outcomes from successfully securitized sectors.

For instance, the reign of Saddam Hussien led to the deployment of weapons of mass destruction and was successfully securitized. Consequently, there were concerns of human right abuse and societal problems which were also securitized. Similarly, the United States and Europe successfully securitized immigration due to the concerns of terrorist infiltration. As a result, extreme measures are applied via tight border controls and the classification of migrants from certain countries of origin, diaspora, emigration and citizenship as potential securitization issues (Naujoks 2015).

The foregoing would have provided a perspective on securitization, and, in order to demonstrate how framing influences perception, it is important to use the example of the 9/11 reportage as a preface to how the media has framed bandits, herdsmen and Boko Haram conflicts in Nigeria. Commenting on the 9/11 media experience, Norris, Kern and Just argue that there was an immediate, post 9/11 "shift in the predominant news frame used by the American mass media for understanding issues of national security, altering perceptions of risks at home and threats abroad" (2003, p. 3-4).

Certainly, this shift affected, and was in part created by journalists. On the surface it appeared that every journalist beat, at least for a time, was reported through a terrorism lens. Not only did reporter routines change to include questions about terrorism after any disaster or crime (Chermak, 2003), but presidential administration and government agency secrecy immediately heightened post 9/11, leaving journalists with a great need to allow additional anonymous sources into their stories in order to do their jobs (Epkins, 2008).

The national security prestige press of Washington, D.C. may operate in a culture unique only to them. Nevertheless, understanding how this "first responder" (Lepre and Luther, 2007) group who can begin the global "media wave" (Fishman, 1980) socially constructs news content is useful to explain the adoption of terrorism news frames, as well as unique routines that may have even spawned from the individual level for this group in particular. The name Boko Haram was given to the terrorist group by the local media, and the international media amplified it.

While not questioning the rationale for this, it is obvious the popularized name, Boko Haram, falls short of what the group stands for. Thus, many scholars have argued that the name is not revealing 'enough' for policy makers to adequately address the ideological challenge posed by it. This shows that the media somewhat wrongly framed the phenomenon of Boko Haram terrorists.

Conversely, field work in North-central states of Benue, Nasarawa, Taraba and Plateau as well as focal group discussions in Kaduna, Katsina and Zamfara reveal a strong view that, whether bandits or herdsmen, the groups are simply terrorists and have strong ties with the Boko Haram. The media and other champions of public opinion have never brought this picture of the bandits and herdsmen to the front burner of public discourse. Thus, the bandits are not identified as a terrorist network or group.

If this were done, it would have probably paved the way for more rigorous

policy formulation in tackling the lingering security challenge. Similarly, herdsmen operated from its inception till 2015 when it was tagged a terrorist group. This only happened when Buchanan (2015) averred that the fourth deadliest known terrorist group has been named as the Fulani militant group operating in Nigeria and parts of the Central African Republic.

It is instructive to say that the declaration of herdsmen as a terrorist group was not done by the Nigerian authorities; rather by the Global Terrorist Index. This betrays the nonchalant attitude with which Nigeria handled the matter. Furthermore, there is no policy rejig by the Nigeria authorities in order to deal with the herdsmen menace. Thus, it still remains a subject of conjecture when this problem will end. Meanwhile, the herdsmen are turning the Benue valley axis of the North-central zone into a killing field.

Regarding the bandits, the framing never linked them to any form of global terrorism. Not until recently that Governor Kayode Fayemi of Ekiti State and the Chairman of Nigerian Governors' Forum (NGF) was quoted by Elumoye (2021) as saying "there is a direct correlation between insurgency in the North-east and what we are seeing manifesting itself as banditry in the North-west or kidnapping in the South-west. Some of the people involved in these are also the ones responsible for insurgency. They are using the resources gained from kidnapping for the activities they are conducting in the North-east. So, we need to take a comprehensive look at all these things and not treat them in compartments. We must treat them as a comprehensive issue and then tackle them collectively."

From the foregoing, it is obvious that framing has played a role in associating the three mentioned armed groups in Nigeria to terrorism. Thus, there has been unequal attention and policy formulation (if any) regarding the fight on crime and criminality that is negatively affecting Nigeria and its people, especially the girl-child. This underscores, therefore, that framing has served a negative purpose in the security situation confronting Northern Nigeria, in particular, and the nation, as a whole.

It is important to remember, that in Chapter One, I attempted defining the ever-difficult concept of terrorism. From the arguments of scholars, particularly Duez (2002), terrorism can be seen through three lenses: the aim, the methods and the expected consequences. Quénivet (2005) criticizes that a definition hinging upon the methods used is rather dangerous, for it means that the definition would depend on the level of technology and creativity of the perpetrators using certain methods.

Van Krieken (2002) simply asserts that "the motives or causes driving the actors are irrelevant", while Sorel dismisses motives as a defining factor on the basis that this enables a common denominator to be more easily found. Lutz (2002), on the other hand, defines terrorism as the use of force for political or religious motives, an approach also adopted by Hirschmann (2003) when analyzing terrorism motivated by ideology or social-revolutionary concerns, ethno-nationalistic considerations, and religion. From the foregoing analysis, Boko Haram and bandits have common methodology as well as socio-revolutionary concerns of marginalization and injustice in the hands of corrupt government officials.

Both are terrorist groups, in my opinion. This is because terrorism implies fanaticism on the part of those involved. Here, I use fanaticism to mean subordination of everything, including life itself, to a single end. The only difference is the religious motivation with which Boko Haram operates. It must be pointed out that religious fanaticism has added a new efficacy to terrorist actions through the legitimization of suicide attacks in terms of eternal reward, in a way that only religion can do.

However, I am aware that not all terrorism is religious in nature, of course. Nor does religion play the same role in all terrorist movements in which it is a significant factor. In Ireland, for example, religion is an important factor in the identification of the two communities in conflict (the Greek Cypriots Islander and Turkish Cypriots Communities), however, it is not the underlying motivation for violence. Another example is that religion does not have any significant role in Basque terrorism in Spain.

The element of religious fanaticism may cause us to lose sight of the complexity of the global terrorism we face today. I do not think that the religious factor in Islamic terrorism is being exaggerated, however, I do feel that we run the risk of excessive concentration on this element to the detriment of other factors, which facilitate emergence and development of terrorist organizations. By excessive concentration on the religious factor, we are simplifying the problem. Religion cannot be isolated as a constituent factor in present-day terrorism from the enormous inequalities that exist.

The unfolding events in Nigeria show that bandits and Boko Haram have the same agenda of terrorism in order to impose strict Islamic religious dogma of shari'a. Thus, bandits, just as Boko Haram, have started attacking churches. An example in view is an attack on a Catholic Church in Kikwari village of Kajuru Local Government Area of Kaduna State during which unspecified numbers of worshippers were killed on February 20, 2021. There was also another attack on

a church in Kaduna on Sunday the 25th of April in 2021, during which a medical doctor was killed along with other worshippers. Though not very clear, it would seem that the bandits also have a religious ideology driving their activities. The pattern of their attacks resembles how Boko Haram started and evolved.

It is important to mention that Boko Haram has not been operating in Niger State, especially recently. However, recent events in Niger State show that Boko Haram and bandits are working together. Buttressing the fact that bandits and Boko Haram are one and have taken over some parts of the Niger State, Governor Sani Bello once lamented, after coordinated attacks on some villages and towns in his state, "I am confirming that there are Boko Haram elements around Kaure in Shiroro local government of Niger State. They have taken over the territory. They have installed their flag. I am confirming to you that Boko Haram terrorists/bandits have taken over some of the wives in the communities and attached them to Boko Haram chiefs. The implication is that the territory now belongs to them" (Asishana, 2021, p. 6).

If bandits are the other side of the Boko Haram coin, it will not be possible for Boko Haram, whose activities in the state have been silent over the years, to suddenly emerge and hoist its flags. It is only bandits that have not given peace a chance in the state, particularly in the past two years. Asishana (2021) reveals that the activities of bandits have led to the displacement of over 3,000 persons and no fewer than 50 villages in five local government areas have been deserted due to attacks by bandits.

SECTION THREE

Boko Haram and Attacks on Educational Institutions

"I Will Never Go Back to School."

– Halima Musa, one of the abducted students in Dapchi.

There is a growing frequency of attacks on educational institutions in Northern Nigeria with farther-reaching effects than meets the eye, especially on girl-child education. Some of the notable attacks include but are not restricted to the following:

- April 14, 2014 – *Government Girls' Science Secondary School, Chibok, Borno State*
- February 19, 2018 – *Government Girls Technical College, Dapchi, Yobe State*
- December 11, 2020 – *Government Science Secondary School, Kankara, Katsina State*
- December 20, 2020 – *Islamiyyah School, Mahuta, Katsina State*
- February 17, 2021 – *Government Science College, Kagara, Niger State*
- February 26, 2021 – *Government Girls Secondary School, Jangebe, Zamfara State*
- March 12, 2021 – *Federal College of Forestry Mechanisation, Afaka, Kaduna State*
- March 15, 2021 – *UBE Primary School, Roma, Kaduna State*
- April 20, 2021 – *Greenfield University, Kaduna State*
- April 25, 2021 – *University of Agriculture, Makurdi*
- April 29, 2021 – *Calvary International Ministry School, Barkin-Ladi, Plateau State*

CHAPTER ELEVEN

Attacks on Educational Institutions

From the foregoing, it is obvious that no level of education – from primary to tertiary – is spared attack. However, what is of particular interest and of worrisome dimension is the target of the girl-child. For instance, of three discovered corpses of the abducted Greenfield University students, two were girls. Furthermore, of the attacked institutions mentioned at the start of Section Three, girls' schools have received more attacks than boys' schools. In the event the attack had been carried out on unisex schools, the girl-child was always the target. This view was strongly canvased at a focal group discussion in Barnawa axis of Kaduna metropolis, three days after the abduction of the Federal College of Forestry Mechanisation students in Afaka, Kaduna.

This subsection focuses particularly on attacks on education and its implication on the girl-child and her education pursuit. It serves a purpose to reiterate that Global Coalition to Protect Education from Attacks (GCPEA 2018) defines attacks on education as any intentional threat or use of force carried out for political, military, ideological, sectarian, ethnic, religious, or criminal reasons against students, educators, and education institutions.

Attacks on educational institutions may be perpetrated by state security forces, including armed forces, law enforcement, paramilitary, and militia forces acting on behalf of the state, as well as by non-state armed groups, as in the case of bandits and Boko Haram. Attacks on schools include attacks on students of all ages, educators, including schoolteachers, academics and other education personnel, members of teacher unions, and education aid workers. Attacks on education also include attacks on education institutions, which includes any site used for the purposes of education at all levels as well as non-formal education facilities, and buildings dedicated to the work of ministries of education and other education administration.

However, for the purpose of this study, attacks on education means activities of Boko Haram and bandits that hinder access to education, particularly for the girl-child. GCPEA (2018) says that a key component of Boko Haram's ideology is hostility toward secular education, and it has gained notoriety for its repeated attacks on schools and universities as well as on teachers, administrators, and students, wreaking havoc on an already fragile education system.

Boko Haram has killed an estimated 2,295 teachers with over 19,000 teachers having been displaced by the conflict. UNICEF (2017) estimates that more than 1,400 schools have been destroyed, damaged, or looted primarily in the North-east, and more than 600,000 children have lost access to education.

In addition to attacking education in general, Boko Haram has specifically targeted female students. What is more, the impact of these attacks on women and girls is often different from that on boys and men. Little wonder, therefore, that Boko Haram gained international notoriety in 2014, when he abducted 276 girls from their school in the town of Chibok. Four years later, more than 100 of the Chibok girls remained in captivity. Chibok, unfortunately, is only one such case. GCPEA (2018) estimates that approximately 600 women and girls have been abducted from their schools. Some of these women and girls reported that Boko Haram had forced them to convert to Islam and subjected them to forced marriage and other forms of sexual and gender-based violence (SGBV).

The abuses committed against female students and teachers as an immediate result of an attack on schools and/or while held in captivity are not relieved once they are rescued or escape. The suffering and impact lingers as girls and young women continue to experience a wide range of harmful repercussions long after the immediate attack.

Attacks on education create a ripple effect, setting in motion a range of negative impacts, such as loss of education, early marriage, early pregnancy, and stigma associated with sexual violence and children born from rape, all of which can dramatically affect female students' futures. These harms are often exacerbated by pre-existing forms of gender discrimination and harmful practices that negatively affect girls and women.

Boko Haram's targeted attacks on schools and the abduction of schoolgirls has harmed female students' access to education. Many of the female students interviewed by GCPEA reported that they had been forced to suspend their education after their school was attacked or had permanently dropped out of school as a result of the attacks. Poverty has been the single greatest obstacle to education in North-eastern Nigeria, and parents' ability to pay for school expenses has been further impeded by the conflict.

In addition to economic factors, many female students interviewed by GCPEA reported that they and/or their parents had been too afraid for them to return to school. Many schools are also closed for significant periods due to insecurity or because the school had been destroyed or seriously damaged during the attacks.

While this study attempts to document numerous abuses that female students and teachers have suffered during an attack on their schools and/or as a direct consequence of such an attack, there are also numerous risks for teenage girls who are not in school, including early marriage, early pregnancy, and lost opportunities for personal autonomy, employment, and economic independence.

While these risks are not limited to girls who have survived attacks on education, girls who attended school prior to an attack are more vulnerable to such risks than they were before the attack.

Many survivors in different focal group discussions held during field work report suffering from mental and physical health problems because of the abuses they have experienced. Some described continuing to endure bleeding and other serious gynecological problems as a result of rape. Many of the students, as well as some of the teachers, described recurring nightmares, anxiety, being easily frightened, an inability to focus, and other signs commonly associated with trauma. Their traumatic experiences often have an impact on their ability to pursue their education and may also impede their ability to move on with their lives in other important ways.

World Bank Group (2016) reveals that before the conflict began, Nigeria had one of the highest rates of child marriage in the world with an estimated 62% of girls in North-eastern Nigeria being married before their 18th birthday and 23.5% before their 15th birthday. The tendency to marry girls at an early age is further exacerbated by attacks on schools that may result in parents taking their daughters out of school or girls, themselves, refusing to continue with their education due to safety concerns. Existential evidence shows that once married, girls often find it difficult to continue with their education due to household responsibilities or opposition from their husbands. Early pregnancy is a further impediment to continuing education, as well as an increased risk of sexually transmitted infections (STIs), exposure to HIV, and a host of pregnancy-related complications.

Meanwhile, there are reports of the girl-child being held in prison-like conditions where they were repeatedly raped. Some ultimately became pregnant as a result. GCPEA (2018) says that some victims, especially those who refused to convert to Islam or marry a fighter, also reported being forced to work long hours for the wives and families of insurgents and being threatened and beaten when they were too exhausted to continue. Some girls and women were forced to participate in or aid Boko Haram attacks.

Another worrisome dimension is that Boko Haram is reported to have used abducted girls as suicide bombers. The United Nations (2017) reported that during 2017, 115 children – 38 boys and 77 girls – had been used as human bombs. That number was six times higher than in 2016. Although difficult to verify, according to Warner and Matfess (2017), those knowledgeable about the Boko Haram insurgency and Nigeria's counter-terrorism efforts believe that many of its child suicide bombers are abductees.

As earlier hinted, targeted attacks on education have remained part of Boko Haram's strategy. Human Rights Watch (2017) reports that approximately 10,000 civilians died in Nigeria between 2009 and early 2016 as a result of Boko Haram's activities. In May 2013, the Nigerian Senate declared a state of emergency in Adamawa, Borno, and Yobe States, leading to increased military activity and an escalation of violence. In August 2017, the IOM (2017) reports that 1,757,288 people were displaced in Adamawa, Bauchi, Borno, Gombe, Taraba, and Yobe States – a slight decrease from previous assessments. The majority of the internally displaced persons (IDP) population (80%) was located in Borno State, and the primary cause of displacement was insurgency.

Boko Haram prevented thousands of children in Borno and Yobe States from continuing their education by destroying schools, driving community members away, and targeting female students in large-scale abductions and other attacks. OCHA (2017) reports that approximately three million children in North-eastern Nigeria were in urgent need of education. In March 2014, Borno State shut around 85 high schools in response to attacks by Boko Haram. Schools in Yobe and Adamawa States were also closed. According to the U.N., 57% of all schools in Borno State remained closed as of late September 2017.

I align myself with the Uzuegbu-Wilson (2018) who argues that attacks on schools violate the right to education enshrined in key international human rights treaties. They also violate international humanitarian and criminal laws and, no doubt, constitute war crimes or crimes against humanity during war or peacetime. For instance, targeted attacks on schools directly contravenes international humanitarian law, which was recognized as a growing concern by the United Nations Security Council Resolution 1612 that reiterated "attacks against schools represent a grave violation against children and are a violation of children's right to education," thus causing irreparable damage to the education of children in terms of "children's access to school and their learning outcomes - and to teachers lives" (Martinez,2013,p.4).

The various types of attacks documented include killings, disappearance, abduction, forced exile, imprisonment, torture, maiming, military use of schools and universities, laying of landmines around schools, and destruction of educational buildings and materials. They also include sexual violence and recruitment and use of child soldiers where it is part of a political, military, or sectarian attack on students or education personnel at or on the way to or from an educational institution (GCPEA 2019).

Attacks on schools occur more often than expected, and one of the major challenges that has further heightened insecurity in the nation is the "ungoverned spaces" often exploited by non-state armed groups. This is because law enforcement capabilities are hindered due to inadequate requirements for the effective control of ungoverned spaces that have suddenly become target zones or safe havens for Boko Haram insurgents and other criminal groups.

Utibe (2016) observes that there is no society that gives adequate attention to their educational growth and development. Nonetheless, in Nigeria, apart from the paltry budgetary allocation by the government, the Boko Haram insurgency has been an obstacle to educational development (Awortu, 2015). By implication, Boko Haram translates to war against Western education, especially in Northern Nigeria.

Terrorists have wreaked havoc in schools, especially those located in Nigeria's North-east. The major targets are primary and secondary schools in the region. According to parents, teachers and human rights defenders from Borno State, many of whom were forced to flee to neighboring states, such as Bauchi, Kaduna and Plateau, nearly all of the schools in the Borno State towns of Bama, Baga, Jajeri, Umarari Garnam, Mai Malari, Mungono and Gamboru were forced to close between February 2012 and June 2013 (ICG, 2014).

Education is under attack in Northern Nigeria. For instance, since the beginning of 2012, according to Amnesty International's research, at least 70 teachers and over 1,001 school children and students have been killed or wounded. At least 50 schools have either been burned or seriously damaged, and more than 60 others have been forced to close. Thousands of children have been forced out of schools across communities in Yobe, Kaduna, Adamawa and Borno States. Many teachers have been forced to flee to other states for their safety (IRIN News, 2013).

In Borno State the attacks destroyed over 882 classrooms as of August 2013, just as in Yobe State, all schools were shut from June to September 2013. On March 6, 2014, the Nigerian Federal Government closed five Federal Colleges (Unity Schools) in Adamawa, Borno and Yobe States, ordering their estimated 10,000 students to relocate (Daily Trust, 2014). According to the Nigeria Teachers' Union (NUT), more than 1,000 teachers have been forced to flee from such areas since 2012. Human rights defenders told Amnesty International that on June 24, 2013, gunmen attacked and killed nine students in the town of Gamboru, Borno State on their way to take their exams.

In a press statement issued on July 6, 2013, UNICEF disclosed that in June 2013 alone, a total of 48 students and seven teachers were killed in four attacks in the region. Between July and September 2013, up to 80 students were reportedly killed by unknown gunmen in two separate attacks in Yobe State. On July 6, 2013 up to 30 people, including at least 25 school children, were killed in their dormitories in Mamudo town, Yobe State. On September 28, 2013, gunmen reportedly killed at least

50 students during an attack on a college in the town of Gujba in Yobe State (Amnesty International Report, 2013).

Again, the kidnapping of about 200 Chibok school children impacts negatively on the image of Nigeria State and the North-east, in particular. Indeed, recent reports have shown that the University of Maiduguri recorded low turnout and those seeking university admission could not select it as a choice due to the upsurge of Boko Haram activities in the area. Parents, fearing attacks, have withdrawn thousands of children/wards from schools in a state that is already the most educationally backward in the country (Awortu, 2015).

In a country struggling with educational infrastructure and qualitative manpower to improve on the standard and quality of education, insurgency by Boko Haram is further compounding its challenges through attacks on the few available schools, kidnapping of schoolgirls, and killing of students and teachers.

Certainly, this is adversely affecting the present and future development of this country. It will further increase the rate of illiteracy in the society for it is an educated and enlightened mind that steers the ship of development (Ugwumba and Odom, 2014). When the rate of illiteracy and school dropout is high, there is the tendency that violence will increase and persist in Nigeria. It is a calculated attempt to create a generation of uneducated youths in the North, so that they can consistently have school dropouts and illiterates to recruit as suicide bombers and fighters.

CHAPTER TWELVE

Abduction of Chibok Schoolgirls

On April 14, 2014, Boko Haram militants attacked a government secondary boarding school in Chibok, Borno State, where girls from surrounding areas had gone to take exams. Their kidnapping sparked one of the biggest global social media campaigns, with tweeters using the hashtag #BringBackOurGirls. 57 of the schoolgirls managed to escape in the immediate aftermath of the abduction, and in October 2016, 21 girls were released after the International Committee of the Red Cross (ICRC) and the Swiss government mediated in the talks between the government and the militant sect (UNFPA, 2016).

Little is known about the fate of the almost 200 girls who are still missing. Even less is known about the thousands of other children who have been abducted in other instances. Hinshaw and Parkinson (2016) are of the view that the numbers are difficult to verify, but there is reason to believe that more than 7,000 women and girls and as many as 10,000 young boys have been kidnapped and many forcefully taken from their schools.

HRW (2016) reveals that, while the girls are forced to marry Boko Haram fighters, raped and even used as suicide bombers, the boys are trained in boot camps in abandoned villages and forest hideouts and later forced to kill their own family and friends. Although some were later rescued by the military, there is reason to be concerned about how the abductees, including children, are treated by the military after release. Some are held in military facilities for months, with little clarity about their status as victims or detainees.

CHAPTER THIRTEEN

Abduction of Dapchi Girls

In the early hours of Tuesday February 25, 2018, no fewer than 50 gunmen from the Islamist extremist group Boko Haram stormed a co-educational, Federal Government boarding school in Buni Yadi, Yobe State, about 65km from the state capital, Damaturu. The attackers locked a dormitory and set it on fire, killing many students inside. Students who tried to escape were shot or murdered in cold blood. In all, there were 59 fatalities; the males were all killed and some female students abducted, while others ordered to quit school and go get married or be killed in future attacks. The school's 24 buildings were completely burned down.

Expanding on an incident previously mentioned, Maclean and Abrack (2018) say that Boko Haram kidnapped 110 girls and one boy from the girls' school in Dapchi, a town in North-east Nigeria, in February 2018 and released most of them a month later after, what the government described as, "back-channel" negotiations. Meanwhile, the only Christian girl among the Dapchi schoolgirls kidnapped by Boko Haram has not been freed along with her schoolmates because she refused to renounce her Christian faith. Her parents learned from snatched conversation with her friends that Leah refused to accept Islam, resisting the entreaties of her classmates to pretend to do so.

Guardian (2021) reveals that three years and five weeks since her abduction in Dapchi, Yobe State, the United States based US-Nigeria Law Group has lamented the plight of the abandoned Dapchi "heroine Christian" schoolgirl, Leah Sharibu, with reports she has given birth to a second child in captivity. It would be recalled that Leah, still held in captivity, was forced to accept Islam before being married off to a top Boko Haram commander after she refused to renounce her Christian faith.

Leah was among the 110 girls, aged between 11 and 19 years, who were abducted by the terrorists from Government Girls' Science and Technical College, Dapchi on February 19, 2018. Convener of the US-Nigeria Law Group, Emmanuel Ogebe, said in a statement that "despite an offer by an American pastor last month to surrender himself in exchange for Leah's freedom, there has been no tangible response from her captors."

While this information is yet to be corroborated by multiple sources, a typically knowledgeable source recently disclosed that she delivered a second child late last year. This means both children were born in 2020 as the terrorists announced one childbirth earlier in 2020. We are still investigating this. As previously discussed, the Guardian newspaper named Leah Sharibu its 2018 "Person of the Year," aptly describing her as "a goddess of resistance."

To commemorate the March 21 third anniversary of the release of the Dapchi girls returned by their captors and "abandonment of Leah Sharibu," the US group, in its commemorative statement, said that until she is released, Leah remains a poster child and symbol of a failed state that can't protect its children. The group also lamented the full scale onslaught on education in Nigeria by Islamist extremists: Boko Haram wars against education, bandits mass kidnapping of children in school, and religious violence against Christian mission school owners in Ilorin over hijab controversy (Guardian newspaper, 2019).

CHAPTER FOURTEEN

Abduction of Jangebe Schoolgirls

According to Olukoya, also in 2021, gunmen abducted 317 girls from Government Girls Junior Secondary School in Jangebe, Zamfara State, a boarding school in Northern Nigeria. Police and the military have begun joint operations to rescue the girls. One of the parents whose daughter was abducted, Nasiru, cited by Olukoya (2021), says that his daughters, aged 10 and 13, are among the missing. Furthermore, Nasiru is reported to have said that "it is disappointing that even though the military have a strong presence near the school, they were unable to protect the girls. At this stage, we are only hoping for divine intervention."

Another resident of Jangebe, Musa Mustapha informed Olukoya that the gunmen also attacked a nearby military camp and checkpoint, preventing soldiers from interfering, while the gunmen spent several hours at the school. It was not immediately clear if there were any casualties. Several large groups of armed men operate in Zamfara State, described by the government as bandits, and are known to kidnap for money and the release of their members from jail.

Nigerian President Muhammadu Buhari said the government's primary objective is to get all the school hostages returned safe, alive and unharmed. I quote him by repeating:

"We will not succumb to blackmail by bandits and criminals who target innocent school students in the expectation of huge ransom payments. Let bandits, kidnappers and terrorists not entertain any illusions that they are more powerful than the government. They shouldn't mistake our restraint for the humanitarian goals of protecting innocent lives as a weakness, or a sign of fear or irresolution" (Olukoya, 2021, p. 2).

Meanwhile, the U.N. Secretary General, Antonio Guterres, strongly condemned the abductions and called for the girls' "immediate and unconditional release" and safe return to their families. He described the attacks on schools as a grave violation of human rights and the rights of children. The U.N. chief reaffirmed U.N. support to Nigeria's government and people "in their fight against terrorism, violent extremism and organized crime," urging Nigerian authorities "to spare no effort in bringing those responsible for this crime to justice." Yet, there is no known arrest and persecution of those involved in the abduction; thereby leaving the citizens with no option for optimism, only a trust deficit in their governments at all levels.

UNICEF representative in Nigeria, Peter Hawkins, is quoted to have said that "we are angered and saddened by yet another brutal attack on schoolchildren in Nigeria." He further explained that "this is a gross violation of children's rights and a horrific experience for children to go through." He called for their immediate release. Anietie Ewang, Nigerian researcher at Human Rights Watch, noted the recent abductions through a tweet that read "strong action is required from the authorities to turn the tide and keep schools safe." Amnesty International also condemned the "appalling attack," warning in a statement that "the girls abducted are in serious risk of being harmed." Teachers have been forced to flee to other states for protection, and many children have had to abandon their education amid frequent violent attacks in local communities (Olukoya, 2021).

SECTION FOUR

Impact of Terrorism on the Girl-child

There are a number of situations that the ongoing violent conflicts in Nigeria, occasioned by Boko Haram, bandits, herdsmen and other forms of violent armed groups, have imposed on the girl-child. Considering the undercurrent culture and tradition of the people, some of the situations go unreported. However, in this subsection, I shall underscore some, with a view to bringing the attention of government and other development partners to the plight of the girl-child.

My concern is that, until and unless critical intervention is undertaken with a view to solving the challenges, the dream of achieving Social Development Goals will remain a mere mirage. It needs reminding that member states of the U.N. (2015) say that "we envisage a world of universal respect for human rights and human dignity, the rule of law, justice, equality and non-discrimination; of respect for race, ethnicity and cultural diversity; and of equal opportunity permitting the full realization of human potential and contributing to shared prosperity."

Furthermore, the U.N. (2015) says that it is working towards "a world which invests in its children and in which every child grows up free from violence and exploitation. A world in which every woman and girl enjoys full gender equality and all legal, social and economic barriers to their empowerment have been removed. A just, equitable, tolerant, open and socially inclusive world in which the needs of the most vulnerable are met." This is a lofty ideal, and the plight of the girl-child in Nigeria seems to demonstrate that it is miles away.

CHAPTER FIFTEEN

Trafficking of the Girl-child

"The Islamic State didn't come to kill the women and girls but to use us as spoils of war, as objects to be sold . . . or to be gifted for free."

– Nadia Murad Basee Taha, a survivor of human trafficking

Cockayne and Walker (2016) say that in December 2015, the United Nations Security Council held its first-ever thematic debate on Trafficking in Persons in Situations of Conflict. Although the connections between sexual violence and armed conflict have become a matter of increasing international concern over the past decade, this was the first time that the Security Council had explicitly addressed the connections between conflict and human trafficking – and what to do about them.

Human trafficking, or trafficking in persons, is defined under the relevant protocol to the U.N. Convention against Transnational Organized Crime to include any form of "recruitment, transportation, transfer, harboring or receipt of persons, by means of the threat or use of force or other forms of coercion, of abduction, of fraud, of deception, of the abuse of power or of a position of vulnerability or of the giving or receiving of payments or benefits to achieve the consent of a person having control over another person, for the purpose of exploitation. Exploitation shall include, at a minimum, the exploitation of the prostitution of others or other forms of sexual exploitation, forced labor or services, slavery or practices similar to slavery, servitude or the removal of organs."

The above underscores the fact that human trafficking in conflict thus encompasses a wide range of illicit conduct, including enslavement, child recruitment, sex slavery, organ trafficking, forced labor and fraudulent recruitment into an armed group resulting in illegal domestic servitude or military service. It is also important to mention from the onset that abduction of women and girls in conflict-affected areas frequently blurs the boundaries between human trafficking and kidnapping for ransom.

Office to Monitor and Combat Trafficking in Persons (2016) acknowledges that armed conflict amplifies the risks of human trafficking for vulnerable populations by increasing economic desperation, weakening rule of law, decreasing the availability of social services, and forcing people to flee for their safety. Armed conflict often results in broken governments, judicial systems, job markets, and community support structures that would normally offer citizens protection from disasters and crime, including human trafficking. Many contributing factors, such as high unemployment rates, homelessness, limited social services, and weak law enforcement oversight, are amplified in conflict zones and exploited by traffickers. Without formal options and services to maintain their livelihoods, people are more likely to resort to illicit activities or risky, informal means to survive, all sectors in which traffickers thrive.

During armed conflicts, governments divert existing resources to respond to the imminent crisis with a resulting loss in facilities and personnel for peacetime governmental services. This exacerbates existing limitations and creates new gaps in a government's structures to protect and provide for its citizens. Some militias use human trafficking to generate income and obtain new combatants. Young women and girls are often forced to marry or have sex with commanders and male combatants. The national and civil disorder caused by such conflict makes traffickers' recruitment tactics — including false offers of jobs, shelter, or education — more enticing to vulnerable populations.

Armed conflict can break down government institutions and create a climate of impunity that encourages traffickers to prey on vulnerable populations. Women and children, migrants, and internally displaced persons are among those most at risk of being subjected to trafficking in conflict zones. The terrorist organization Boko Haram, for example, has abducted and forced women and children into sexual slavery in Nigeria, and the Somali National Army continues to recruit children into combat (Office to Monitor and Combat Trafficking in Persons, 2016).

Corroborating this view, Adepelumi (2015) argues that more than 1.5 billion people live in countries affected by violent conflict. Conflict is a push factor for trafficking, migration and poverty. In Nigeria's prone conflict zones, Boko Haram trafficked children and used them as soldiers and militias. They kidnap young girls then sell them into slavery and/or forcefully marry them. This is why the United States Department of State (2016) says that armed conflict amplifies the risks of human trafficking for vulnerable populations by increasing economic desperation, weakening rule of law, decreasing the availability of social services and forcing people to flee for their safety.

Camps for refugees and internally displaced persons are prime targets for traffickers.

The concentration of vulnerable, displaced people combined with the lack of security, services, and oversight typically found in such camps, make them ideal locations for traffickers to operate. In long-standing camps, traffickers are able to build relationships with corrupt camp officials and establish trafficking rings.

Office to Monitor and Combat Trafficking in Persons (2016) further explains that human trafficking is frequently overlooked in crises and omitted from formulations of humanitarian and emergency response policies. Trafficking operations can flourish amidst international reconstruction efforts where there are few government institutions or rules of law. The international community and individual countries must recognize labor and sex trafficking as a common occurrence during conflict and include anti-trafficking strategies in humanitarian responses.

Meanwhile, Human Rights (2020) says women and girls continue to be exploited in sex trafficking, reportedly by other IDPs, aid workers, and low-level government employees. Some charges were brought against government officials, security force members, and other perpetrators. For example, a Nigerian Air Force officer was convicted, dismissed and sentenced in 2019 by a court-martial for sexual exploitation of a 14-year-old girl in one of the IDP camps. In August he was turned over to civilian authorities for further criminal prosecution. In September a military court-martial, convicted, dismissed from service, and sentenced a soldier to five years' imprisonment after he raped a teenage girl in Borno State.

Furthermore, it is reported that children (younger than age 18) participated in Boko Haram attacks. The group paid, forcibly conscripted, or otherwise coerced

young boys and girls to serve in its ranks and perpetrate attacks and raids, plant IEDs, serve as spies, and carry out PIED bombings, often under the influence of drugs. The group also subjected abducted girls to sexual and gender-based violence, including rape and forced marriage (Human Rights, 2020).

Cockayne and Walker (2016) consider human trafficking within and into conflict areas to include sexual exploitation, other forms of enslavement, forced labor and forced military service. Tragically, today the Islamic State of Iraq and Levant (ISIL) (Da'esh) and Boko Haram both openly advocate the enslavement of women and children in direct defiance of international law and norms. For instance, Nigeria's Child Rights Act of 2003 provides extensive protection for children in conflict situations and the right to free, compulsory, and universal primary education. It also prohibits abduction of children, child labor, sexual abuse and exploitation of children.

Despite the above legislation in addition to other international instruments that Nigeria is a signatory to, the situation of protection against human rights abuse and trafficking has remained abysmally poor. For instance, Human Rights Watch (2016) says that between 2009 and October 2014, Boko Haram abducted more than 500 women and girls. Furthermore, Mausi (2017) reveals that women and girls abducted by Boko Haram are forced to marry, convert, and endure physical and psychological abuse, forced labor, and rape in captivity.

Victims are threatened with whipping, beating, or death unless they convert to Islam, marry their captors, stop attending school, and wear the veil or hijab. Human Rights Watch (2016) worries that another attack on Zanna Mobarti Primary School in Damasak, also in Borno State, on November 24, 2014 led to the abduction of an estimated 300 young students. So far, none of these children have been returned to their parents. It is very probable that they have been trafficked.

According to Human Rights Watch (2010), trafficking of Nigerian women for prostitution to Côte d'Ivoire and other countries in Central and West Africa continues to be of concern. Human Rights Watch further states that many victims are between the ages of 15 and 17. Scores of similar cases involving Nigerian women and girls were documented by Ivorian officials, United Nations personnel, and Nigeria embassy staff. In 2016, the US State Department highlighted ongoing concerns about trafficking of Nigerian women to Cote d'Ivoire and other West and Central African countries, as well as South Africa.

Human Rights Watch (2010) confirms the presence of five separate brothels of Nigerian women and girls in two small towns in central Côte d'Ivoire, with populations of about 40,000 and 50,000 respectively. Human Rights Watch investigations indicated that the majority were likely to have been trafficked. All the women and girls interviewed by Human Rights Watch described being promised work as apprentice hairdressers, tailors or other businesses elsewhere in West Africa or Europe. Nigerian women recruited and transported them overland through Benin, Togo, Ghana, and Burkina Faso.

What remains to be seen is the action of the Nigerian government that goes beyond lip service in an attempt to address the situation. This action must include, as a matter of necessity, social security and good governance that will lme the challenge of corruption that has stifled drastic implementation of laws. The Nigeria state must treat crime as the name implies, while at the same time build institutions that are responsive to their mandates.

For instance, in 2015, Nigeria was ranked 152 of 188 in the United Nations Development Program's Gender Equality Index, which gauges gender parity (UNDP, 2015). Although there is gender discrimination throughout the country, it is particularly acute in the North. UKAID (2012) says that one out of every three women in Nigeria reported having experienced some form of violence, including physical, verbal, emotional and psychological abuse, marital rape, sexual exploitation, or harassment within the home. Boko Haram and bandits have worsened the existing bad situation.

CHAPTER SIXTEEN

Sexual Abuse and Gender Based Violence

The United Nations (1995) defines gender-based violence (GBV) against women as any act that results or is likely to result in physical, sexual, or psychological harm or suffering to women, including threats of such acts, coercion or arbitrary deprivation of liberty, whether occurring in public or private life. However, it is instructive to say that the term also applies to violence specifically targeted against men and boys (UNFPA, 2012: 3).

Russo and Pirlott (2006) point out that the definition of gender-based violence emerged from the 1995 United Nations Conference on Women in Beijing. It represents an international consensus on how to conceptualize the dynamics of gender-based violence and encompasses child sexual abuse, coercive sex, rape, stalking, and intimate partner violence.

The term "gender-based" is used because such violence is shaped by gender roles and status in society. Gender-based violence against women does not encompass every violent act a woman may happen to experience (being threatened by a weapon during a robbery, for example). A complex mix of gender-related cultural values, beliefs, norms, and social institutions implicitly and even explicitly have supported intimate partner violence and provided little recourse for its victims.

In particular, gender roles and expectations, male entitlement, sexual objectification, and discrepancies in power and status have legitimized, sexualized, and helped to perpetuate violence against women, rendering it invisible (Russo and Pirlott, 2006).

One of the ways that gender has shaped the meaning of violent acts against women and men is by differentially conferring legitimacy on male violence against women. With legitimacy has come invisibility for the victims. Marriage, as a social institution, has come under particular scrutiny for providing men an entitlement to batter and rape their wives, providing legitimacy for their actions. Ironically, it was not until the late 1980s that intimate violence became identified as the leading public health risk to adult women by the surgeon general of the United States (Koop, 1985).

The invisibility of male violence against women is truly remarkable given its pervasiveness and profound health, social, and economic consequences. With the rise of what has become a global women's movement, the legitimacy and invisibility of such violence became challenged. Today, male gender-based violence against women is globally recognized as a health, economic development, and human rights concern (Amnesty International, 2004).

A comment cited in OHCHR (2008) observes that "it has probably become more dangerous to be a woman than a soldier in armed conflict." This assertion is predicated on what Barstow (2000, p. 3) said. According to him "the ratio of military personnel killed to civilians killed has changed from 8:1 in World War I to 1:8 in wars after 1945." The majority of the victims are women, children and the elderly. This is the worrisome reality that wars and violent conflicts have brought upon women and children.

It is a sad reality that sexual violence has always occurred during armed conflicts at all times. This happens in a pertinacious manner despite the fact that International Criminal Law (ICL) has made sexual violence in conflict a violation of the Rome Statute. In a focal group discussion with elderly women in Kokki in Shiroro local government of Niger State, it was revealed that no age group was spared sexual violence.

Women of all ages are targeted and sexually violated, especially raped, around the clock. Often, the women are killed right after such atrocities are committed. But since 'dead bodies don't talk' there is little or no mention of this for the public to know. There are similar stories of this nature in the Baki axis of Borno State.

Human Rights (2020) reports that Boko Haram engaged in widespread sexual and gender-based violence against women and girls. Those who escaped, or whom security services or vigilante groups rescued, faced ostracism by their communities and had difficulty obtaining appropriate medical and psycho-social treatment and care. In 2019 Boko Haram kidnapped a group of women and cut off their ears in retaliation for perceived cooperation with Nigerian and Cameroonian military and security services.

Therefore, it would suggest that bandits and Boko Haram are using sexual violence as a weapon of war. This is because women and girls are particularly targeted by the use of sexual violence, including as a tactic of war to humiliate, dominate, instill fear, disperse and/or forcibly relocate civilian members of a community, particularly the girl-child. The aim is to ensure that the girl-child is made to be unstable and, thus, not in a position to have any form of education thereby achieving the overall objective of Boko Haram towards prohibition of Western education.

It is important to mention that during raids on unsuspecting community members, especially women and the girl-child, anonymity becomes a curse rather than a blessing. For instance, key informants said that it is easier to sexually violate a woman when she is anonymous than it is to do to someone the male knows.

The scenario of the ongoing violent conflict in Northern Nigeria provides the needed context for the terrorists because the bandits or members of Boko Haram do not know the women they rape and neither does the women know them. For them, she is simply treated as an impersonal entity that has only one right: to provide them with sex and nothing more.

A focal group discussion with escapees revealed horrifying experiences. According to them, their time with Boko Haram was marked by near-daily Quranic education, training in how to be suitable wives for the insurgents, strict gender segregation, and punishments imposed by a rigid interpretation of Sharia law mandating corporal punishment for violations.

The abductees reported that they were given little food and experienced sexual violence followed by marriage to the insurgents where they were expected to have sex with their husbands. Many of the women who escaped suffer from trauma, post-traumatic stress disorder (PTSD), and other mental health challenges.

Another shocking revelation is that young men and boys in the sect, both voluntarily and by force, are trained in horrifying ways to perpetrate violence against their communities. Communities throughout the country's North region tell stories of young men and boys who are forced to kill members of their own family—even parents—as a sort of initiation ritual (Blueprint, 2017). Murdock (2014) says that by making them kill their own parents or their own family, it puts them in a position where they can't go back. Psychologically, they are absolutely broken. They killed their parents. They literally murdered those who brought them to life. In that sense, their loyalty becomes to the only family that they have now, which is the army or the terrorist group that kidnapped them.

Even those who have been merely exposed to violence report trauma.

Not only does this violence undermine social trust, it traumatizes those (especially the children) exposed to these acts and fosters a notion of masculinity and power that is intrinsically linked to violence. Blueprint (2017) observes that extreme subservience of women and girls and the acquiescence of violence against them deeply affect not only the victim but also those forced to witness and perpetrate such acts. Children who are deeply traumatized by exposure to violence become more vulnerable to perpetuating it. As long as these attitudes are held, women are not safe. Across a number of countries, rates of domestic violence spiked at the end of conflicts.

Legal Defence and Assistance Project (LEDAP) cited in Inwalomhe (2021) reports that women and girls in the Boko Haram infested North-east are randomly raped in exchange for food and water. The Project said that the incidents occurred mostly in the host communities and the Internally Displaced Persons (IDPs) camps located in Borno, Adamawa, Yobe States and Abuja, the Federal Capital Territory. There are several reports of sexual abuses, including rape and exploitation of women and girls living in many internally displaced person camps in Borno, Yobe, Adamawa States, Chad, Niger Republic and Cameroon.

Legal Defence and Assistance Project analyzes information collected from over 325 respondents in Borno, Adamawa, Yobe, and Abuja, which indicates high incidences of recurring sexual and gender-based violence, forced child marriage and sexual exploitation in exchange for food and water, which occurs with impunity in IDP camps and host communities.

One woman sums up her experience with these haunting words: "I have been raped so many times that I can't even remember." Several women and girls, including pregnant women, were raped, more often than not, in the presence of their children, and many contracted HIV after these experiences and yet they are yet to obtain any justice.

There are different typologies of gender-based violence. However, these varying forms can be coalesced into the following:

- Overt physical abuse (includes battery, sexual assault)
- Psychological abuse (includes deprivation of liberty, forced marriage, sexual harassment)
- Deprivation of resources needed for physical and psychological well-being (including health care, nutrition, education, means of livelihood)
- Treatment of females as commodities (including trafficking)

Zenn and Pearson (2014) argue that Boko Haram have always treated women as pawns. Thus, they disclose that Boko Haram carried out a series of kidnappings in which one of the main features was the instrumental use of women in response to corresponding tactics by the Nigerian government. Kidnapping is a recent development for the group, and the first suggestions of this tactic emerged in Boko Haram statements in January 2012. It was then that the group's leader, Abubakar Shekau, issued a video message threatening to kidnap the wives of government officials in response to the government imprisoning the wives of Boko Haram members (Associated Press, 2012).

However, Boko Haram's first actual kidnapping operation was carried out one year later in February 2013, with the abduction of a seven-member French family in northern Cameroon that they brought back to Nigeria (The Guardian, 2013). The family group included four children. Between February and May 2013, the kidnapping strategy was brought directly to Nigerian soil, with the abductions of more than a dozen government officials and their families in Boko Haram's main base of Borno State.

In May 2013, Boko Haram carried out a mass assault on a police barracks in Bama, Borno State in which militants captured 12 Christian women and children (Agence France-Presse, 2013). The arrest of Boko Haram members' wives triggered an aggressive reaction of kidnapping of women and girls. According to Zenn and Pearson (2014), the capture of Boko Haram militants' family members was cited as a grievance in almost all Shekau's video statements in 2012 and 2013. In his first statement after the mass detentions, Shekau explicitly accused the government of "kidnapping" women (YouTube, 11 January 2012). Subsequent video messages reiterated this theme, with complaints of a sustained government strategy of arrests of Boko Haram family members.

When, in mid-September 2012, the government detained an additional 10 women associated with Boko Haram, Shekau responded with his fifth video message, which was made public on September 30, 2012. In it, Shekau threatened revenge on wives of government officials. He also speculated on the possible sexual abuse of the Boko Haram family members by security forces, when he said "...they have continued capturing our women. In fact, they are even having sex with one of them. Allah, Allah, see us and what we are going through" (YouTube, September 30, 2012). In that same video, he made clear the intention to target 'enemy' women in return. "Since you are now holding our women, (laughs) just wait and see what will happen to your own women... to your own wives according to Sharia law."

These events demonstrate an established cycle of government detentions of women related to Boko Haram, and the group's retaliatory abduction of Christian women. All these women were targeted for instrumental purposes, as none of those captured on either side had any direct involvement in the conflict.

CHAPTER SEVENTEEN

Out-of-school Situation of the Girl-child

"Keep away from schools or we'll kill you,"

– Shekau warned.

In recent years, the North has suffered continuous attacks by Boko Haram and bandits. Their activities, according to Outhred and Turner (2020), has led to over three million internally displaced people, disrupted agricultural production and decimated educational infrastructure and activities in the North-east zone.

Furthermore, terrorist activities have exacerbated the socio-economic disparities between Northern and Southern Nigeria. Even prior to the terrorist insurgency, approximately 34% of school-aged children in the North did not have access to basic education, and the region usually ranked lowest on most socio-economic and educational indices (UNICEF, 2015).

Despite encountering fewer direct effects of the insurgency than the North-east, the North-western zone has seen substantial disruption of services caused by migration from the North-east and the notorious activities of bandits. Research undertaken by the World Bank found that out-of-school rates for 6 to 11 year-olds in the North-west were 53% and 43%, for girls and boys respectively compared with 31% and 25% nationally, as reported by Nigeria Partnership for Education Project (2015).

Outhred and Turner (2020) observe that in the North-west, 20% – 33% attend non-integrated Qur'anic schools and are, therefore, considered out of school (they do not cover the mainstream curriculum) while the rest of those counted as being "out-of-school" (i.e. the remaining 20% – 33%) have never attended any form of school. Recent estimates show that the sub-Saharan Africa region accounts for 52% of the global out-of-school children. 22% of primary school-age children in sub-Saharan Africa are out-of-school.

Nigeria's Demographic and Health Survey (NDHS) data for 2008 shows that some 7.3 million children of primary school age were out of school. When the junior secondary school component is taken into account, the out of school children (OOSC) problem becomes even larger, with wide regional, geographical and gender disparities across the country. Even when enrolled, hundreds of children (especially girls) are not showing up for class.

Outhred and Turner (2020) argue that, although girls' primary school attendance has generally been improving, this has not been the case for girls from the poorest households. So many children drop out of primary school that the expected Junior Secondary School (JSS) enrollment rate is very low. Thus, Nigeria's major challenges are low attendance, low completion rates and gender as well as regional/ geographical disparities.

Femi (2011, p. 103) says that "about 46,340,000 Nigerians out of about 140 million cannot read or write."

UNICEF (2006) estimates that approximately 93 million children of primary school age are not attending school, and out of these, 48.5 million are girls. UNICEF further revealed that Nigerian children, some of whom either had not formally attended school or had dropped out of school, are engaged in various forms of labor either for their education or to support their family households. Specifically, Nigerian children work in the following occupations: Street vendors (64%), Beggars (13%), Foot washers (8%), Car washers (6%), Scavengers (5%) and Shoe shiners (4%) (UNICEF, 2009).

In a more recent study than Femi's, the World Bank (2015) tells us that Nigeria has an estimated 13.2 million school-age children (6 – 14 years old) not in school– the largest out-of-school population in the world. Of the 13.2 million, fully 12.6 million (95 %) are in the North, reflecting a clear North/South divide.

The ongoing conflict in Northern Nigeria has undoubtedly exacerbated the systematic drivers behind low school attendance in the region. Relying on different sources, Ayantunji (2019) says a recent report by Sahara Reporters states that over 1,400 schools have been destroyed since the start of the Boko Haram insurgency in 2009. Also, The Punch newspaper reported, in a special edition in 2018, that over 2,295 teachers have been killed in the different attacks by insurgents in the Northern part of Nigeria.

In the World Economic Forum's (WEF) "Global Competitiveness Report," they said, "Nigeria ranked 122nd out of 138 countries for quality of primary education and 136th out of 138 for primary education enrollment as a percentage of the total population" (WEF, 2016, p 283). Free, basic education was passed into law in 2004, but parents are still expected to pay for uniforms, materials and transport. Poverty is thus reported to be the main barrier for school attendance. With more than 50% of the population in the North-east living below the poverty line (World Bank, 2014) many families cannot afford these costs.

Other underlying factors to why Nigerian children are out of school as identified by EDOREN, (2016) include ethnicity, religion, geography and disability. Ayantunji (2019) argues that barriers to girl-child education in Nigeria, especially in the North, have been tied to several factors such as poverty, early marriage, cultural and religious misconceptions or misrepresentations as well as teenage pregnancy.

This aptly summarizes the major problem we have in the Northern part of the country, which has Bauchi State leading the chart with about 1,239,759 students out of school due to the different reasons and circumstances stated previously.

Being a girl from the poorest household in the North-east of the country means your chances of going to school are meager. If you also have a disability, you will most likely never obtain your right to education. Before the uprisings started in 2009, 72% of children age 5 – 16 had never attended school in Borno State, the hardest hit area of the crisis. Literacy rates were as low as 28% across all the North-eastern states, compared to 52% for the whole of Nigeria (National Education Data Survey, 2010). Differential access to education is demonstrated to be a driving factor behind the growing inequality in Nigeria.

Insurgency and acts of terror have, by no small means, dampened the enthusiasm of children to go to school and embedded in parents the fear of sending them. Economic barriers and socio-cultural norms and practices also discourage attendance in formal education, especially for the girl-child. Mandela cited Adamu (2018) who says an educated, enlightened and informed population is one of the surest ways of promoting the health of a democracy. Essentially, education is an equalizer that gives citizens choices, strengthens the office of the citizen, and develops the critical minds needed to question duty bearers and bring them to account, which is essential for social justice.

Education is a vital tool for combating poverty, empowering women, protecting children from hazardous, exploitative labor, and sexual abuse as well as promoting human rights and democracy. These are the gains that education delivers. However, the ongoing insurgencies in Northern Nigeria will not rob the region of these gains alone, but other accompanying multiplier effects will also take root. It is rather sad that Boko Haram and, by extension, bandits have walled the girl-child from education for obvious reasons. The activities of these armed groups have plummeted school enrollment and worsened retention.

For instance, from the reliable data gathered by Health Policy Training and Research Programme (2018) school attendance was about 70% in 2011 but reduced to 60.9%

by 2016. Between 2016 and now, the situation has geometrically deteriorated, thereby robbing the earlier gains achieved. By this, it would appear that Boko Haram has achieved its aim of resisting the spread of 'Western education.' Furthermore, it is a known fact that out-of-school children are at an increased danger of abuse, exploitation and recruitment into bad behavior, including becoming radicalized and joining insurgent groups.

Arising from several factors of the ongoing conflict, some parents become weary in educating their female children. Mallam Akilu Abubakar Mayanchi, whose children were abducted at Government Girls Science School (GGSS) in Jangebe, Talata Marafa Local Government Area of Zamfara State, remains a megaphone for such parents when he averred that "from now on, my daughters will be withdrawn from the Western education system" (Mahammed and Olagoke, 2021, p. 6). He further laments that "Western education is over for my daughters" (Mahammed and Olagoke, 2021, p. 1).

The mindset of Mallam Akilu is a reflection of the general feeling gathered in most parts of the North. It would be a double tragedy for a region, already over- weight with the burden and lack of education for the girl-child, to slide into the unfortunate dungeon of educational oblivion. It will, therefore, require the intervention of relevant stakeholders to protect the girl-child and give her the tool of education for her to be a competitive global citizen of the 21st century.

It is argued in some quarters that the government has been responding through a number of strategic interventions intended to improve enrollment by addressing the issue of accessibility. Efforts are also underway to better retention and achievement by improving quality and reducing inequalities and paying greater attention to gender sensitive and inclusive policies, as well as instituting more effective education management systems.

Accessibility is being addressed through an increased number of schools within reach of populations. Other remedial measures include provisions for teacher development, making education more easily affordable, flexible programs for children from nomadic communities, reduction of socio-cultural barriers and the introduction of social welfare measures. However, the desired result is yet to be seen.

SECTION FIVE

Insecurity in Nigeria and Global Politics

What is playing out in Nigeria is much more than the failure of the Nigerian government to handle its internal affairs. There are indicators of possible external factors that are germane to how Nigeria is perceived or has acted as an international player. Therefore, there are pundits who are of the view that the ill-wind of globalization is affecting Nigeria in all ramifications. The critical questions begging for answers are, "Does Nigeria understand the enormity of this and will it portend to its well-being and future?"

Is Nigeria playing the proverbial ostrich amidst its drowning plight? These are some of the issues that shall be interrogated; with the purpose of understanding how they have all affected and effected the current insecurity plaguing the nation that is sometimes described as the giant of Africa. My concern is that in all these issues, what is the guarantee of the safety and well-being of the girl-child?

CHAPTER EIGHTEEN

The Diplomatic Angel of Insecurity - Possible Reasons for Nigerians' Woes?

As of today, Nigeria faces many security challenges, some of which are rooted in diplomatic trappings. In this section, I shall examine the security challenge posed by Islamic Movement of Nigeria (IMN), popularly known as Shiites, and the alleged Iranian desire to destabilize Nigeria.

Zenn (2013) says a former Iranian diplomat described the IMN as an Iranian proxy. Evidence has shown the IMN serves as an extension of Iranian foreign policy in Nigeria. This is substantiated by the track record of the IMN akin to Hezbollah. For instance, a former career diplomat (who defected and is now living in Europe), who previously served as Iran's consul general in Dubai and was an adviser to the Iranian foreign ministry, said the IMN was set up by and modeled on the Lebanese Hezbollah and that Iran provides the IMN with training "in guerrilla warfare: bomb-making, use of arms, such as handguns, rifles and RPGs, and the manufacturing of bombs and hand-grenades" (Assadinia, 2015).

Providing a clearer perspective on how Iran has perfected its tact of using proxies, Zenn (2013) argues that Iran's activities in Nigeria are consistent with its actions throughout Africa. For example, in Kenya, two members of the Quds Force were found guilty in May 2013 of storing explosives and carrying out surveillance of Israeli, British, U.S. and Saudi targets (Odula, 2013).

Levitt (2013) explains further that the Nigeria and Kenya plots fit the pattern of Quds Force and Hizb Allah operations involving Iranians and dual Lebanese-European or Lebanese-Canadian nationals that targeted Israelis in India, Georgia and Thailand in February 2012, Azerbaijan in March 2012, and Cyprus and Bulgaria in July 2012.

These incidents suggest that Iran has always used proxies on its target. The failures of all but the Bulgaria cells, as well as the ability of Israeli intelligence to help national governments track them, may have prompted Iran to search for new targets in Africa in 2013, such as Kenya and Nigeria, where Israelis often travel and conduct business (Zenn, 2013).

Africa is usually hoodwinked into some of these traps via aid. For instance, while Iran has increased economic activities and aid to Africa in recent years, much of Iran's influence is won through ideology promotion, as seen with the IMN in Nigeria. For instance, Kamara (2004) is suspicious of the opening up of Iranian Cultural Centres (similar to Confucius Institutes or Alliance Francaise) in countries, such as Sierra Leone and Tanzania. According to him, this is an attempt to convert villages from Khartoum to Kordofan in Sudan to Shi'ism, and invited Ivorian and Sudanese Shi`a imams to the Basij base in Ramshir, Southwestern Iran.

In a related development, Ridgeon (2012) argues that indigenous African Shi'a (as opposed to Lebanese-West African citizens) in Sierra Leone, Senegal and other countries receive funding to study Shi'ism in Lebanon or Iran and return home sympathizing with "Khomeinism." The former president of Comoros from 2006 to 2010, for example, was even nicknamed "Ayatollah" because he studied in Qom under Ayatollah Mesbah-Yazidi, the mentor of former Iranian President Mahmoud Ahmadinejad (BBC, 2006).

It is based on the foregoing that Zenn (2013) posits that just as in Nigeria, some African Shi'a have become militants, such as the Ivorian who, in July 2013, became the "first African martyr" in Syria defending President Bashar al-Assad's forces and was later eulogized by Hezbollah. Although the IMN does not promote violence, its imams preach that the West conspires to "dominate minds and resources" of Muslims by converting them to Christianity and secularizing them. They also believe that Jews are the "lowest creatures on earth" and the "children of monkeys and pigs."

Gudaku and Bulus (2020) say that on December 12, 2015, the IMN and Nigerian State's Chief of Army Staff's (COAS) convoy clashed with the Shiite procession in Gyallesu at Zaria. The clash erupted into violence where the army fired several gunshots at the procession, and, subsequently, the house of El-Zakzaky and Husainiyyah were invaded and destroyed by the army (Report Afrique 2015). More than 300 people were reported killed, including the wife of El-Zazzaky and top Shiite leader of the Kano branch, Sheikh Mahmud Turi, among others. (Leadership 2015).

Doukham (2016) says that, "Iranian authorities accused Saudi Arabia's coalition with the U.S. and arrogant powers is a blatant example of friendship of blasphemers; the Saudi king's congratulations to the perpetrators of Nigeria's crimes is shameful and disgraceful [...] in a country where Boko Haram kills innocent people and takes children and women as slaves and no effective measure is taken against it, they treat 15 million Muslims in a violent manner only for fulfilling their religious duties and staging protests against Israel."

Iranian authorities took severe measures and summoned Nigeria's chargé d'affaires to express its outrage at the Nigerian military's deadly crackdown on Shiite Muslims, including the arrest of Sheik El-Zakzaky the leader. The chargé d'affaires informed the Nigerian Foreign Ministry that Iran demanded that the Nigerian government "immediately shed light on the incident, treat the injured, and compensate for damages."

Additionally, Sweene (2015) reveals that Iranian Foreign Minister Mohammad Javad Zarif called for the immediate and serious action to prevent violence against Shiites in a telephone call to his Nigerian counterpart Geoffrey Onyeama. For Anjide and Chukwuma (2017), the different opinion of Iran and Saudi Arabia is not surprising because of the Shiite and Sunni divide in the Middle East. I find this objectionable and misleading. The reason is that the theological polemics between Shiites and Sunnis, alone, is not enough to elicit the aforementioned contradictory reactions from Iran and Saudi Arabia.

After all, as Doukham (2016) posits, Muslims are split into two main branches, the Sunnis and Shi'a. However, members of the two sects have co-existed for centuries worldwide and share many fundamental beliefs and practices. In addition, the theological feud between Shi'a and Sunni is too cold (due to many years of existence) to warrant the kind of steam coming from the duo of Iran and Saudi Arabia.

Therefore, it is curious to ask, why has such fierce disagreement not emerged between Iran and Saudi Arabia in other places where such similar incidents have happened? This underscores the conviction that the conflicting reaction is due to existing competition between Iran and Saudi Arabia as to who bears the flagship of global Islamic hegemony. The reactions should be understood in the context of socio-political interest. It is against this background that Doukham (2016) insists that Iran is seeking to create a 'Tropical Shi'a Zone' as part of the 'Shi'a Crescent' within its aspiration for regional hegemony and become a global superpower recognized in any geopolitics negotiations.

The Iranian nuclear program, the subversion in foreign countries, and the support given to terrorist organizations should be regarded as tools utilized by Iran to further its intermediate objectives of becoming a global superpower. Of course, the Nigerian state will logically come under vicious attack from Iran because it is hob-nobbing with countries, such as the USA, that Iran considers a foe.

The continued undermining of the Nigerian state and her institutions by the IMN came to its crescendo with protests in Abuja, the nation's capital, including in the Three-Armed Zone, where the legislature, judiciary and executive (Presidency) are headquartered. The protests occasioned the death of many citizens, including a deputy commissioner of police, Usman Umar, and a 21-year old serving member of National Youth Service Corps (NYSC), and Precious Owolabi of Channels Television, both of whom were undertaking their lawful duties. The massive protest by the group explained why Justice Nkeonye Maha of the Federal High Court in Abuja issued an order, following an ex parte application.

The court restrained any person or group of persons from any form of activities involving or concerning the IMN under any name or platform in Nigeria. The Federal Government published the order proscribing the IMN in the official gazette on July 29, 2019 (The Nation, 2019). Hitherto, in a short video that went viral, Governor Nasir Ahmad el-Rufai of El-Zakzaky's home state of Kaduna accused the group of refusing to participate in any democratic process in Nigeria. According to him, members of the IMN do not register for voter's cards and, thus, do not vote.

This seems to confirm the insinuation that the group is desperate to create an Islamic state in Nigeria. In addition, members of the IMN do not pay taxes, and yet, use government facilities, such as schools and highways that are funded from taxes collected by the government for demonstration. To further show that the IMN is a government within the sovereign nation of the Federal Republic of Nigeria, El-Rufai has revealed that the IMN have appointed their governors and Local Government Chairmen across the federation. It is to these appointees that members of the IMN owe their allegiance, not to the government of Nigeria and all her arms. In addition, members of the IMN do not subscribe to the national anthem and have no recognition for the national flag or public holidays. Rather, they have their own flag and public holidays.

Security and Diplomatic Concerns Zenn (2013) reveals that Iran's Quds Force and Hizb Allah's global operations have involved Nigeria for more than a decade, but their activities were exposed in October 2010. Nigerian customs officials in Lagos seized 13 containers of weapons from a ship operated by the same French-Lebanese businessman's company that, in March 2011, saw a ship bound for Sinai, Egypt via Syria to supply weapons to Hamas in Gaza that was intercepted by Israeli naval commandos.

Revealing the details of the arms, Tattersall (2010) says the containers included 107mm Katyusha artillery rockets used by Hezbollah against Israel in 2006. They were shipped on behalf of a Tehran-based Islamic Revolutionary Guard Corps (IRGC) "front company" and picked up at Bandar Abbas in Iran where the IRGC has a naval base (Adebowale, 2010). Top security sources informed Zenn (2013) that the weapons were destined for a warehouse in Abuja, but shippers altered documents to send them to Gambia (presumably for anti-Senegalese rebels in Casamance).

Nigerian security officials arrested four individuals: a senior Quds Force officer; a

Nigerian who formerly studied in Iran and worked at Radio Tehran's Hausa language service; and two Nigerian customs officials. A fifth Iranian suspect, Sayyed Akbar Tabatabaei, who was the Quds Force Africa Corps commander, took refuge in the Iranian Embassy, flew back to Tehran with Iran's foreign minister and was reportedly reassigned to Venezuela to run Quds Force operations in Latin America (Vanguard, 2011).

Demonstrating the deep involvement of Iran, Reuters (2013) reported that one month after these arrests, $10 million worth of heroin hidden in auto engine parts was suspected of being linked to the weapons shipment in October that was seized in Lagos from a ship originating in Iran. However, this was a late discovery because, as hinted by Mohammed (2013), Iran's role in weapons trafficking resurfaced in May 2013 when Nigerian security forces uncovered a weapons "armory" in a Kano home owned by the Lebanese consul to Sierra Leone.

The security forces arrested three individuals, all of whom admitted to receiving training from Hezbollah, including a Lebanese citizen, who owned a supermarket and amusement park in Abuja; a second Lebanese citizen, arrested at the airport in Kano before boarding a flight to Lebanon; and a dual Lebanese-Nigerian citizen. Although the weapons were rusted, Nigeria's director of the State Security Service said they were "serviceable," and a Nigerian brigadier general said they were intended for attacks on U.S. and Israeli targets in Nigeria (Pointblanknews.com, 2013).

According to Sahara Reporters (2012), some of the munitions, such as anti-tank mines, are more compatible with rebel groups than a terrorist group and may have been linked to the weapons and heroin shipments in Lagos in 2010. Odo (2013) reveals that in February 2013, three months before uncovering the "armory," Nigeria announced it also uncovered an Iranian-funded cell whose leader admitted to plotting attacks on "prominent Nigerians" to "unsettle the West." Such leaders included Nigeria's former military leader, Ibrahim Babangida, and former Sultan of Sokoto, Ibrahim Dasuki, as well as Saudi Arabia's ambassador to Nigeria (Vanguard, 2013).

Furthermore, Adigwu (2013) says that the cell also conducted surveillance on USAID, the Peace Corps, an Israeli shipping company, a Jewish cultural center and hotels frequented by Americans and Israelis in Lagos. Some of those involved were identified. For instance, Nwogu (2013) points out that the cell's leader, a Shi`a imam in Ilorin, attended a course at Imam Khomeini University in Qom in 2006. In 2011, he trained in the use of AK-47 rifles and improvised explosive devices in Iran. In 2012, he travelled to Dubai to receive funding to form the cell (Daniel, 2013).

The foregoing has grave implications for security in Nigeria. For instance, the proxies being used can become security threats to the country. As is often argued, the worst enemy is the person who presents himself/herself as a friend. Therefore, Nigeria needs to appraise her diplomatic ties and change her policy direction with nations that use proxies to undermine her internal security. This is fundamental, especially considering that the nation is littered with internal violent conflicts of varying magnitudes.

The proscription of the IMN has been greeted with mixed feelings from analysts.

While some support the action, others are suspicious about it. For instance, Adibe (2019) has advanced seven reasons why the group need not be proscribed. The reasons included the fear of what Iran, through other means, will do in its continued hunt of Nigeria because of its bilateral alliance with Iranian foes, such as the USA and Israel. However, the position of this paper differs from Adibe's view. The reason is that Nigeria, as a sovereign state, stands to lose more if it allows itself to be a pawn in the chess game of Iran in its quest to actualize its hegemonic quest.

CHAPTER NINETEEN

Global Politics After 9/11

There are events that have drastically changed world affairs and the way individuals, and even nations, relate. D'Abadie (2003) says some of these events range from the dropping of the A-bomb in August 1945 to the Treaty of Rome in 1957 to the Munich Olympics and the international prominence of terrorism in 1972 to the emergence of oil as a weapon in 1973 to the rise of political Islam in 1979 to Chernobyl and the importance of the undisputed recognition of a political dimension for the environment in 1986 to the fall of the Berlin Wall in 1989. Another defining event is the 9/11 attack on the United States.

D'Abadie (2003) says that, since the shock from the September 11, 2001 terrorist strikes on the US, the widespread belief is that the world is no longer the same and the character of international politics and security have radically evolved. The terror strikes on the US's East Coast have undeniably compelled the international community to realize that overt threats have been replaced by considerations of "risks" and "challenges" and that the international environment is based no longer on the management of security but on the management of insecurity.

Transnational dimensions have assumed a salient profile in societal evaluations as considerations of stability and security and, in this perspective, 9/11 has led the US to adopt a more radical, uncompromising approach in its foreign and defense policy to take account of the new definition of security and the more diffuse notion of contemporary challenges, including asymmetrical threats.

Stevens and Vaughan-Williams (2014) observe that the events and aftermath of 9/11 have presented, what some analysts consider to be, a new world order in terms of threat perceptions. Namely, it has 'resulted in chronic changes to schematic representations of the social world as a dangerous and threatening place for many people', giving a 'new urgency to understanding the degree, origins, nature and consequences' of threats.

The securitization of migration and its increasing association with transnational crime and international terrorism – particularly, though not exclusively, in Europe and North America – is just one example of "new politics" and "new security" issues since 9/11. At a time when attempts have been made to 'conscript' ordinary members of the public into the state's security apparatuses, and national security strategies make a virtue of involving citizens in the risk management cycle, it is more important than ever to understand public perceptions of security threats and their role in contemporary political life.

Yet our knowledge of public perceptions of security threats tends to be confined to discrete policy areas, such as terrorism, or relates to specific areas of personality, predispositions or attitudes, such as authoritarianism and tolerance. Thus, Stevens and Vaughan-Williams (2014) say that the persistence of an elite focus in security studies means that we still know relatively little about the range of issues that individuals regard as security threats, as well as their causes and the levels at which such threats are perceived, for example, as global or national threats.

This study, during focal group discussion, had citizens offering alternatives to what needs to be done in order to end the ongoing violence in the country. The different views collected can be coalesced in a manner that suggests that the insurgency has turned the socio-political landscape of Nigeria into a proverbial plantation, where the girl-child is harvested (abducted) as if she is some kind of food crop. This ugly situation urgently calls for the rejigging of Nigeria security architecture as well as its diplomatic relations.

CHAPTER TWENTY

Using Diplomacy and Security for the Safety of the Girl-child in Northern Nigeria

The history of the diplomacy framework of Nigeria cannot be complete without reference to the founding fathers, particularly Sir Abubakar Tafawa Balewa. Ajaebili (2011) argues that it was at the U.N. on October 8, 1960 during his speech Sir Balewa spoke about the cardinal principles that would underpin Nigeria's foreign policy, and scholars have generally agreed that the basic principles of the pronouncements are as follows:

i. **The Principle of Non-Alignment:** The policy of non-alignment rejects formal alliance with the existing ideological and military power blocs of the Capitalist West, led by the United States, and the Communist East, led by the Soviet Union, in the post-World War II international system. This policy was adopted by Nigeria and other newly independent states of Africa and Asia to help promote international peace and security in view of the Cold War conflict between the two superpower blocs of NATO and the Warsaw Pact.

ii. **Legal Equality of States:** Nigeria adopted the principle of respect for the legal equality, sovereignty and territorial integrity of all states designed to protect the small and newly independent states from the domineering influence of the developed nations. Moreover, the principle of legal equality underscores the assumption that all states are equal in the comity of nations with equal opportunity to advance their views and interests through the media of International Organizations.

iii. **Non-Interference in the Domestic Affairs of all other States:** Nigeria upheld the principle of non-interference in the internal affairs of other countries. Duringthe Nigeria Civil War of 1967 – 1970, the then General Gowon's regime maintained that the war was an internal affair and therefore vigorously discouraged other countries from encouraging the secession of Biafra (Njoku and Nwafor, 2005).

iv. **The Principle of Multilateralism:** This implies the freedom to seek membership of both continental and global multilateral organizations. Membership of these International Organizations will enable Nigeria to pursue its interests and contribute to the common goals of the organizations.

v. **Africa as the Cornerstone of Nigeria's External Relations:** As stated, Africa has been the centerpiece of Nigeria's foreign policy since Independence. And in the pursuit of this Afri-centric foreign policy, it has assisted liberation movements in various parts of the continent, thereby dismantling the last vestiges of colonialism. Besides, Nigeria has shown commitment in the implementation of this policy through efforts at peaceful resolution of conflicts on the continent "and the championing of the struggle to uplift the socio-economic well-being of the African through continental programs, such as the New Partnership for African Development (NEPAD) and African Development Bank (ADB) assisted sustainable economic development programs (Njoku and Nwafor, 2005, p. 39).

The thrust in Nigerian foreign policy has been Afri-centric in nature. The use of Afri-centric rather than Afro-centric, which is more popular in literature, is deliberate. This decision is predicated on a citation credited to Bennett (1967: 46). According to him, "at the Racism in Education Conference of the American Federation of Teachers, the delegates unanimously endorsed a resolution which called on all educators, persons, and organizations to abandon the 'slavery-imposed name' 'Negro' for the terms 'African American' or 'Afro-American'." Given this old association of the root term "Afro" in making reference to the "identifiable Americans of African descent," I therefore prefer, in the context of this discourse, to use the term Afri-centric in making allusion to Afri-centricism order to give it the proper African connotation it deserves.

In order to demonstrate its Afri-centric foreign policy pursuit, Nigeria had intervened in peace-keeping in different African countries. Buttressing this view, Dauda et al (2017) say that Nigeria's role in the maintenance of peace and stability in the African continent is great due to its Afri-centric policy. Nigeria has taken part in numerous peace-keeping and peace-making processes in the continent.

Osimen et al (2015) also agree that the contributions of Nigeria to international peace-keeping operations cannot be over emphasized since her independence from Britain in 1960. Nigeria became a prominent actor both within and outside the international system. Nigeria, by all standards, is committed to regional peace and global security, despite the fact that the world is highly conflictually structured as a result of technological advancement, specifically in the Western world.

Scholars, particularly Osimen et al (2015), argue that Nigeria first provided U.N. peacekeepers to Congo (ONUC) from 1960 to 1964. Since then, Nigeria has been an active participant in U.N. peace-keeping missions, deploying military contingents, unarmed military observers, and military staff officers, as well as having formed police units and provided police advisors and civilian experts to over 25 U.N. missions.

Nigeria is currently one of the largest U.N. contributing countries with military and civilian personnel deployed in 10 U.N. peace-keeping operations and the African Union Mission in Somalia (AMISOM). Nigeria has also played pivotal roles in other non-U.N. missions in Africa. As the preponderant power in West Africa, Nigeria has been the main provider of military and other resources for ECOWAS peace operations to the tune of $8 billion in its various missions in Cote d'Ivoire, Guinea-Bissau, Liberia, Mali, and Sierra Leone.

During the peak of the Liberian and Sierra Leonean civil wars in the 1990s, Nigeria provided over 70% of the Economic Community of West African States Monitoring Group's (ECOMOG) military and civilian personnel, as well as logistical support. In 2003, it deployed 1,500 troops to the Economic Community of West African States' (ECOWAS) Mission in Liberia (ECOMIL), a medical and signals team to the ECOWAS Mission in Cote d'Ivoire (ECOMICI) in 2003. In 2004, 1,500 Nigerian troops were deployed in Darfur as part of the African Union's (AU) Mission in Sudan (AMIS). Recently, Nigeria also provided 1,200 troops to the African-led International Support Mission in Mali (AFISMA), and 200 police officers to the African Union Mission to Somalia (AMISOM).

Nigeria deployed the first set of individual police officers (IPOs) in Africa to the United Nations Operation in the Congo (ONUC) in 1960 while the pioneer Formed Police Unit (FPU) of 120 officers was deployed in Liberia in 2004 (Osimen et al, 2015).

The security challenges generated within individual societies spread across borders to their surrounding environment and are exacerbated by unhealthy regional dynamics. In the Western hemisphere, narcotics syndicates originate on one side of the world, but target and exploit vulnerable societies on the other side. The current security threats encompass challenges to human security and a whole series of social and environmental degradation along with traditional military security challenges. And they occur in a time of bewildering connectivity and advancing political complexity as the world becomes increasingly and simultaneously interlinked and multi-centric, thereby justifying the intervention by Nigeria.

Sule (2013) argues that Nigeria has also been using the mechanism of peace- keeping to translate her inspirational quest for African leadership into reality. Its contributions to the Peace Support Operation (PSO) have contributed to boosting the country's military and diplomatic status within the international system. It has been through the instrumentality of the peace-keeping force that Nigeria has assumed the status of a major actor in international conflict management.

Arising from peace-keeping, more African countries, and the outside world, have come to appreciate the centrality of Nigeria to African affairs. Nigeria has shown commitment to promoting international peace and security through her participation in PSO. The country has particularly demonstrated her ability when conducting sub-regional PSO missions. Consequently, Nigeria has leveraged on her peace support role as a basis to claim a seat in an expanded U.N. Security Council.

Meanwhile, the role of Nigeria in peace-keeping was acknowledged even by Western powers that positioned the country as a regional hegemon. This position is considered by her neighbors as an enviable one. It also reawakened the traditional rivalry of colonial masters over their colonies. The Francophone, according to a focal group discussion in Abuja, started using their proxies and colonies, who are neighbors of Nigeria, to undermine her security. As to whether this has vexed the Anglophone remains unclear. But since then, Nigeria has never remained the same. Its unity has consistently come under threat.

Nigeria is arguably one of the largest economies on the African continent.

Thus, the country is seen as a forerunner of continental development and epitome of regional diplomatic links in West Africa, thereby posing a regional hegemon. This is because Nigeria has made concerted efforts to position itself as a critical global actor in international political and economic relations. Conspiracy theories are rife that Nigeria's rising influence has become a threat to its neighbors and other distant envious nations. Therefore, no one is particularly interested in genuinely helping to resolve the country's increasing security challenges. Little wonder that Hassan (2015) is of the view that the international hegemonic policies, which have long scrambled for African resources, have shown that it is quite unlikely for an African nation to rise as a strategy-imposing superpower in the current transformative post-Cold War era.

According to Yilmaz (2010) the term hegemony, originating from ancient Greek 'hegemonia', literally expresses the dominant and oppressive status of one element in the system over the others. The concept of hegemony greatly contributes to a better understanding of current international and power relations. Antonio Gramsci has significantly contributed to the articulation of this concept suggesting that power is not only dependent on force but also on 'consent.'

However, Antoniades (2008) contends that the concept of hegemony may imply a great capacity for coercion and/or a great degree of influence or control of the structures of the international system and the international behavior of its units, but it excludes situations where we have the establishment of relations of direct and official control of foreign governments or territories.

Along these lines, for instance, we can distinguish the concept of hegemony from the concept of colonization (which implies direct, official control). Thus, hegemony differs from any form of relationship that implies direct management or ownership of foreign territories. Consequently, the concept of hegemony does not cover forms of domination, such as annexing, occupation or acquisition of foreign territories or population.

Historically, the term hegemon signified "leadership" or "sovereign ruler." The term expanded to include the military, economic, and political dominance of one nation state over another, for example: Ur, Athens, Corinth, Portugal, Britain, and the United States (Herrmann, 2017). The move towards a hegemonic position in West Africa is rather a bane than a blessing for the country.

Intriguingly, Gudaku and Ogah (2019) observe that in 2006, an espionage arm of United States intelligence apparatchik, the Central Intelligence Agency (CIA), released a report titled 'Mapping the Global Future' that predicted the disintegration of Nigeria by 2015. Mixed reactions greeted this report from within and outside the country. As reactions to the report continued to reverberate, what followed was diplomatic denials and counter-denials. For instance, Awolaja (2014) says that, while speaking with the media in Ibadan, the former US Ambassador to Nigeria, Mr Terence McCulley, is quoted to have insisted that the US never predicted that Nigeria would break up by 2015, claiming that the prediction was made by a private agency that carried out a survey, not the US government.

Despite this denial, the factors mentioned in the CIA's report accounting for the possible break-up of Nigeria have continued to raise their ugly heads, thereby making the prediction more of a reality than a myth. For it is as true today as it was when the National Intelligence Council's 2020 Project Report (2014) warned that, while Nigeria's leaders are locked in a bad marriage that all dislike but dare not leave, there are possibilities that could disrupt the precarious equilibrium in Abuja. Of most importance would be a junior officer coup that could destabilize the country to the extent that open warfare breaks out in many places in a sustained manner. The National Intelligence Council's 2020 Project Report (2014) further cautioned that, if Nigeria were to become a failed state, it could drag down a large part of the West African region.

Gerald and Cletrence (2013), in another security report entitled, 'Nigerian Unity in the Balance', again warn Nigerian leaders to beware of another civil war or an outright breakup. They are particularly worried that, having already experienced one brutal civil war, Nigeria is at risk for a recurrence of conflict or dissolution, especially since some of the underpinning motivations of the war remain unresolved.

In all these reports, the following are identified and itemized as the fault lines of the possible disintegration of the country: Ethnic and regional bias; historic Christian-Muslim rivalry; pandemic insecurity and terrorism; corruption and impunity as well as the inability of state authorities to live up to its statutory responsibilities.

At the National Confab of 2014, delegates were antagonistically divided along regional lines of North and South. For instance, the Lamido of Adamawa at the National Confab threatened the nation with cessation. More damming is the new phenomenon that has never been since the history of Nigeria. At the threshold of the 2015 elections, some states, particularly Imo in the South-east and Kano in the North- west, threatened to undertake the registration of Nigerians who are not indigenous to the mentioned states. Aside from the unconstitutional clout of the action, the whole exercise, even before its execution, had widened the yawning divide of North and South.

For example, Emmanuel (2014) observes that, vexed by the plan to register Northerners in Imo state, Arewa Youth Development Foundation had called for peaceful dissolution of Nigeria and issued a two-week ultimatum for Southerners residing in the North to relocate southwards, while Northerners should abandon their dwellings in the Southern part and return to North. In response, the Ohanaeze Youth Council had made no pretence of calling off the bluff, not only of Arewa Youth Development Foundation but also the Arewa Consultative Forum, the socio-political umbrella body of the North. This development was worrisome, to say the least. In addition, it gave credence to the 2015 US breakup prediction theory.

Though Nigeria survived the 2015 mark line of potential separation, the country remains more divided than ever. It is simply a shadow of its old self, with Boko Haram and bandits fueling the ongoing conflicts in different parts of the country.

While the government is calling on the international community for assistance, key stakeholders are of the view that Nigeria cannot be helped.

For instance, the British Minister for Africa, James Duddridge, has described Nigeria's security situation as massively complex, stressing that no partnership would resolve the multiplicity of the country's problems, whether it is Boko Haram insurgency or a number of other issues. Duddridge made the comments while responding to questions from journalists attached to Nigeria's ministry of foreign affairs. The UK government has stated that partnership cannot help the Buhari-led administration tackle insecurity in Nigeria (Ukwu, 2021).

In the UK, you have a strong partner across the full gamut of issues. So, it's not just about intelligence and hard security and military, it's about societies, humanitarian support, education and development partnership.

The paradox and dilemma is for Nigeria to look inwards rather than outwards for solutions. However, there seems to be no silver lining in sight (at least at the moment). The reason is that, instead of tackling this situation dispassionately, the political leadership is stuck in a blame game that provides no clear solution to the issue. Furthermore, corruption and lack of the required hardware are hampering the operations of the security agencies fighting to keep the nation safe. While this lasts, the plight of the girl-child continues to be worsened.

Acknowledgements

First and foremost, I want to express my profound gratitude to my God who sustains me; and to Reverend Sister Mary Bulus, Anthony DeAngelis, Noreen Costello, H.E Ambassador Prof. Joy Ogwu, Dr. Noreen Leahy, Jim Leahy, Benjamin Tyavkase Gudaku, Ralph Poli and Thomas Gilman who help the dear Lord in this task every day.

Next, I wish to express my appreciation to the following: priests whose prayers and support are always felt; Rudy Gonzalez, David Simone, Charles Udokang, Charles Romano, Lawrence Onyegu, Emmanueal Patrick, Bret Stockdale, Joseph Mali, Benjamin Zirra, Sr., and to my priest spiritual directors over the years, Fr. Peter Ali Yakubu, Fr. Jacob Yali, and Fr. Mike McNamara, you have made priceless contributions towards my success in life, and I thank you. Thanks to the late Archbishop Gabriel Gonsum Ganaka, Archbishop P.Y Jatau, and Bishop Joseph Danlami Bagobiri who were instrumental in my journey to the United States.

I especially wish to express my gratitude and appreciation to my editor Lauren Mix, to my academic professors who have skillfully introduced me to a more profound understanding of the principles of International Affairs and Diplomacy; Prof. Zhang Wang, Fredline McCormack-Hal, Sara Moller, Purnaka De Silva, Aaron Hale, David G. J. Wood, Zenaida Miller, and to Professor Gary Schenellert, Jared Kengwe, Jude Asiegbu, John Souza, Dr. Ada Menaokika, Dr. Devon Bannister, Prof. Peter Bauna-Tanko, Dr. Louis Yaah, and Prof. Joseph Mammon, without your guidance this book would not have been created.

I also wish to extend my appreciation to Senator Danjuma S. Laah, H.E Rt. Hon Dr. Phillips Phinn Anderson, UN Volunteers Ambassadors SDG-VSDR Department of Northeast Affairs at the United Nations, the Hon. Bruno F. Romano, and Hon. Allan Beach, the mayors of East Rockaway and Lynbrook for your encouragement and support.

I am deeply grateful to Deacon Bob Zeuner, Eugene Quast, Maria Reasa, Astride Fidelia, Rita Chojnaki, Richard & Linda Horan, and Berta Forero, Mathew Pignatoro, and Timothy J. Hoffman for your help and encouragement and making me a better priest. I extend my sincere gratitude to the Most Rev. Dr. Julius Yakubu Kundi home Bishop to Bishops, George Dodo of Zaria, Mathew Hassan Kukah of Sokoto, John Nyring of Kano, Stephen Mamsa Dami of Yola, and Damen of Maidugri, the Sisters of Our Lady of Apostles, Admiral Peter Ebhaleme, Joseph E. Nyere Ph.D., Andrea Bartoli, Cardinal Joseph Tobin, and the Oblate of Nazareth Sisters for always believing in me. I wish to express my deep love and appreciation to you all.

I will always remain grateful to Fr. Amos Barack, Philip Kwasau, Timothy Dogo, Wilfred Dodo, Lawrence Taja, the late Sylvester Gimber, Mathias Peter, Williams Abba, Basil Akut, and all the class of 1995 from St Augustine Major Seminary for sharing this journey with me. To Courtney Smith, Martin S. Edward, Daniel Kristol, Nancy Gardner and Shaunta Toote, thank you for taking a special interest in my progress. I am indeed highly indebted to Bishop John Barres and Bishop Christopher Cardone for their willingness to take a chance in me.

To my friends, Emmanuel Anigbogu, Donatus Anigbogu. James McCabe, Kit Evelly, Kevin Schaefer, Alcira Herz- Shoemaker, Friedrick Charles Shoemaker, Herman A.Mahecha, Lucy Ferraro, Edmund Zukowski, Doreen Dolan, Sarah McAteer, Seaon P. Dolan, Lucille Pulglissi Vetrano, Kathleen Russo, Victoria Leo Gambo, Wilfred Anigekwu, Admiral Peter Ebhaleme (Rtd), Benjamin Sabiyi (Rtd), Philip Hassan Moses, Esther Bishen, Patricia Nyan, Susan A. Malcolm, Rev Sarah Raymond, North Dakota; thank you for the moral support.

To my co-workers Sr. Ruthann Gypalo, Sr. Lorraine Studley, Evelyn Contaldi, Lucy Osterman, Terry Leonetti, Mary Fehey, Louis Diez, Jacob M. Hoffman, Louise Mario, Michael Sloan Sr, Michael Sloan Jr., Mary Thomas, Steve Bermuzede, Paul Kahl, Robert C. Campbell, Thomas Connolly, Guy Donza, Richard W. LaRosa, Thomas J. Malone Jr, Thomas Donza, Laura Garbitelli, Ann Marie Lynch, Steve Bennett, Linda Ohlsen, Dorothy Bock, Patricia Winterand, Michael Carver, Alice Schenkel, and Alisan Fererra for making each day a joy for me.

To Alfred Babarino, the Sodality Women's Organization of St Raymond's in East Rockaway, NY, the Knights of St Columbus Council Rockville Center Diocese, Melisa Abuin, Patrick and Audrey, Bosede Naomi, Aladi Bulus, Vincent Cerrato, Vierge Benjamin, Gina Mesola, Louis Deiz, Jacob Hoffman, Keith & Kim Bui, Dr. Theodore Illoh, Dr Cine, Fr Lawrence Onyegu, Dr. Joseph Maiyaki, Karryri Kura, Dinna Jjei, Sokad Usa, Dr Sarah Philip, Eunice Gankon, Esther Bishen, Shantel, Nigerian Catholic Community NY, Germain Leviet, Dr. Patrick Adekola, Vierge Benjamin, Dr. Maryanita Anderson, Anne Petraro, Joseph Petraro, Oswald Hyppolite, Kevin

O'Keefe, and Gina and Maria Mazzola, Theresa Gaffney, Elizabeth V. Halpin, Chinedu Patrick Nwaneri, Anthony Vitta, Ifota Kadimba, Jacinto DaSilva, George Mello, Lauline Mello, Fatima Louro, Manuel Lauro, Diana Santos, Manuel Anthonio, Albina Anthonio, Emmanuel Patrick OSA, Nuhu Bature HRH, Andrew Kazaha -Allahmagani HRH, Bala Ghuga HRH, Bala Ghuga HRH, Thaddeus -Abubakar Bulus, Simon Pama Bulus, Ibrahim Sabastine Bulus, Rapheal Ayafe Bulus, Salama Bulus, Anthony Awuni Jatau, Emmanuel Arbiriyi, Sr Caroline Alibo, Sr. Florence Golam, Sr Mary Patrick, Sr Martine Olf, Charles Romano, Bishop John Barres, Archbishop Timothy Michael, Cardinal Dolan, Mary Collins, Bishop Nicholas DiMarco, and Bishop Robert J.; Thank you for your friendship and belief in me.

Finally, I wish to thank those I may have forgotten to mention. Know that you are loved and prayed for every day.

About the Author

Vincent Hassan Bulus is a Roman Catholic priest of the Diocese of Kafanchan, Nigeria. He is an academic scholar who has contributed to both local and international journals while lovingly attending to his flock. His care, especially for the sick and dying, explains why he has served as a hospital chaplain and is the founder of a Non-Governmental Charitable Organization, the Hope-Yet Center for Empowerment (HYCE), where he attends to the needs of the underprivileged and marginalized.

Dr. Bulus obtained his Bachelor's degree in Sacred Theology from the Pontifical Urbanian University - Rome Affiliate - St. Augustine Major Seminary, Jos in 1995; and his Doctorate in Philosophy from the University of North Dakota Grand Rapids in 2012. In between, Dr. Bulus obtained three Master's Degrees; a Master's of Science in Higher Education and a Master's of Science in Educational Leadership both from St. Cloud State University, Minnesota in 2008, and a Master's of Science in Diplomacy & International Relations from Seton Hall University, New Jersey in 2020.

Dr. Bulus has been the recipient of many awards and grants from different reputable organizations, including the United Nations in 2014. Dr. Bulus is also a member of numerous Organizations and Associations, including the Black Students Association of North Dakota (BSA), the Association of Catholic Chaplains (CPE), the Association of International Educators (NAFSA), the Association for the Prevention of AIDS in Africa, and the Knights of Columbus Minnesota, to name a few.

In February 2021 Dr. Bulus was appointed special Peace Ambassador for the City of New York by WOLMI-ECOSOC of the United Nations and awarded an Honorary Doctor of Divinity Donor Causa from CICA International University & Seminary, Houston Texas in 2019.

He has also completed numerous academic certificates in the following fields and specialties:

- Policy Analysis, University of North Dakota (UND) 2018
- Multilateral Diplomacy and Negotiations, Unitar 2020
- Protocols and Diplomacy, WOLMI Diplomacy Academy 2021
- Humanitarian Diplomacy, 2021
- Chaplain Leadership and Ministry, CICA International Houston Texas 2020
- United Nations Studies School of Diplomacy & International Relations
- International Strategic Crisis Negotiation Exercise, 2021 US War College/ NYU School of Professional Studies Center for Global Affairs

Dr. Vincent Bulus's research interests include participatory democracy, international security, peace and conflict resolution and gender equality.

His concern for individual freedom, dignity, and the liberation of women at all levels is what gave birth to this book.

Dr. Bulus is currently serving as an Associate Pastor at St. Raymond of Penyafort R.C. Church in East Rockaway, New York.

About the Foreword Author

Prof. U. Joy Ogwu has spent the greater part of her life in disarming, quiet, unobtrusive service to her country teaching, mentoring young scholars, raising young leaders, conducting research in International Relations, and representing Nigeria at the highest levels.

Ambassador Uche Joy Ogwu is an exceptional scholar, author, administrator, and diplomat who left an indelible mark on the institutions and processes of global security, conflict resolution and peace-making.

A distinguished Professor of Political Science and International Relations, she served as Minister of Foreign Affairs of Nigeria (2006 - 2007), the first female Permanent Representative of Nigeria to the United Nations (2008 – 2016), Director-General, and Nigeria's Foreign Policy Think-Tank – Nigerian Institute of International Affairs (2001-2006).

At the UN, she served as Member UN Advisory Board on Disarmament Matters (2002), First African Chair of the Board from 2006 – 2007, First President of the First Executive Board of UN Entity for Gender Equality and Empowerment of Women, as well as Four-time President UN Security Council.

In recognition of her meritorious services to the nation and humanity, Prof. Ogwu has won several national and international honors, including award of Officer of the Federal Republic (OFR) in 2004. She serves on the Governing Board of Nigerian Prize for Leadership (NPL), Chairing the NPL Committee on Strategy and Foreign Relations, the Boards of Baze University Abuja, and the Pan African Institute for Global Affairs and Strategy (PAIGAS), Abuja.

Works Cited

Abdullahi, A. (2019), 'Rural Banditry, Regional Security, and Integration in West Africa'. Journal of Social and Political Sciences, 2 (3): 644-654.

Abimbola, J.O. and Adesote, S.A. (2012), 'Domestic terrorism and Boko Haram insurgency in Nigeria, issues and trends: A Historical discourse.' Journal of Arts and Contemporary Society, 4 (1), 11-29.

Adamu, M. A. (2018), "The implications of out-of-school children". Retrieved from http://out%20of%20school%20children/out-.html on 03/18/2021.

Adebowale, Y. (2010), "Illegal Weapons Loaded in Iran". This Day, October 29.

Ademola, A. (2021), "The Growing Threat of Armed banditry in the North-West". Retrieved from http://www.STRIFE.html on 03/24/2021.

Adibe, J. (2019), IMN: 'What does it mean to be a terrorist organisation'. Daily Trust, Thursday, August 1.

Adigun, B. (2013), 'Nigeria Secret Police Say Terror Group Broken Up'. Associated Press, February 20.

Agence France-Presse, 13 May 2013, "New Boko Haram video claims attacks, shows hostages", via http://mg.co.za/article/2013-05-13-new-boko-haram-video-claims-at- tack-shows-hostages. Accessed 9/1/2014.

Ahmed, L. (1992). *Women and Gender in Islam: Historical Roots of a Modern Debate.* New Haven: Yale University Press.

Ajaelibi, C. N. (2011). 'The Option of Economic Diplomacy in Nigeria's Foreign Policy.' International Journal of Humanities and Social Science, 1 (17), 270-280.

Aju P. C. and Aju, J. A. (2018). 'Occupation of Sambisa Forest and Boko Haram Insurgency in Northeastern Nigeria as Security Threat and Challenges to Sustainable Forest Management'. Global Journal of Science Frontier Research: Agriculture and Veterinary, 18 (5), 22-31.

Akosim, C., Alo, E. B. and Mbayu, Y. P. (2015). 'Investigation of Soil Characteristics of Sambisa Game'.

Alabi, T. and Alabi, O.S. (2014). 'Female education: A sociological analysis of girl-child education in Nigeria'. Int. J. Educ. Policy Res. Rev. 1 (1), 006-013.

Albert, I. O. (2017). *Beyond Nigeria's Sambisa: Forests, insurgency and counterinsurgency in Nigeria.* Ibadan: Ibadan University Press.

Aljazeera, (2020). "Five killed by gunmen in northwest Nigeria Mosque attack: Police". Retrieved from www.aljazeera.com, on 06/20/2020.

Alubo, O. (2006). *Ethnic Conflict and Citizenship Crises in Central Region, Programme on Ethnic and Federal Studies.* Ibadan: University of Ibadan Press.

Amnesty International (2004). *It's in our hands: Stop violence against women.* Osney Mead, Oxford, United Kingdom: Alden Press.

Andrew, O. and Etumabo A.G. (2016). 'The Implications of Girl-Child Education to Nation Building in the 21st Century in Nigeria'. Global Journal of Human and Social Science, 16 (3), 1-4.

Antoniades, A. (2008). 'From 'Theories of Hegemony' to 'Hegemony Analysis' in International Relations'. A paper presented at the 49th ISA Annual Convention Panel: Hegemony, Security, and Defense in International Relations, San Francisco USA, 28 March.

Anyadike, A. (2021). "The Longshot bid to rampart banditry in Nigeria's Northwest." Retrieved from http://www/BANDITARY/the%20new%20humanitarian.html, on 25/03/2021.

Asishana, J. (2021). 'Boko Haram has taken territory in Niger, says governor.' The Nation, Tuesday, April 27.

Assadinia A. (2015). "Will Iran's proxy go to war in Nigeria?". Retrieved from https:// www.linkedin.com/pulse/irans-proxy-go-war-nigeria-daniel-brett-msc-fras, on 08/ 05/2020.

Awolaja, A. (2014). "Nigeria and 2015 Prediction" Nigerian Tribune, May 29.

Awortu, B. E. (2015). 'Boko Haram Insurgency and the Underdevelopment of Nigeria,' Research on Humanities and Social Sciences, 5 (6): 213-220.

Ayantunji, O. (2019). "Tackling the Out-of-School Children Menace in Nigeria; A Foundation's Systematic Solution." Retrieved from http://out%20of%20school%20 children/o-sch.html, on 01/24/2021.

Ayoub, M. (2007). A Muslim View of Christianity: Essays on Dialogue by Mahmoud Ayoub. Omar, I. A. (Ed.). Orbis: New York.

Bagu, C. and Smith, K. (2017). *Past is prologue: Criminality and reprisal attacks in Nigeria's Middle Belt, Washington, DC: Search for Common Ground.*

Barstow, L. A. (2000). *War's Dirty Secret: Rape, Prostitution, and Other Crimes Against Women.* Ohio: Pilgrim Press.

Benford, R. D and David A. S. (2000). 'Framing Processes and Social Movements: An

Overview and Assessment', Annual Review of Sociology, Vol. 26: 611–639

Berman, H., Straatman, A., Hunt, K., Izumi, J. and MacQuarrie, B. (2002). *Sexual harassment: The unacknowledged face of violence in the lives of girls.* In H. Berman & Y. Jiwani (Eds.). *In the best interests of the girl child.* Ottawa, Ontario: Status of Women Canada.

Blench, R.M. (1998). *The status of the languages of Central Nigeria.* In M. Renzinger (Eds.). *Endangered languages in Africa.* Köln: Köppe Verlag.

Blueprint, (2017). "Futures Without Violence: Linking Security of Women and Security of States". Retrieved from http://www.EDUCATION%20AND%20GBV/FWV_blueprint_8-Boko-Haram.pdf, 03/21/2021.

Bockstette, C. (2008) "Jihadist terrorist use of strategic communication management techniques," in George C. M. Centre Occasional Paper. Retrieved from http://www.marshallcenter. org/mcpublicweb/MCDocs/files/College/F_Publications/occPapers/occ-paper_20-en.pdf

Brownmiller, S. (1975). *Against our will: men, women and rape.* New York: Fawcett Books

Buchanan, R. P. (2015). "Global Terrorism Index: Nigeria Fulani Militants named as fourth deadliest group in the world." Retrieved from www.independent.co.uk, on 04/08/2021.

Chermak, S. M. (2003). 'Marketing fear: Representing terrorism after September 11.' Journal for Crime, Conflict, and the Media, 1(1): 5-22.

Church of the Brethren, (2020). "EYN churches are attacked, at least 12 people are killed, a pastor/evangelist is among those abducted in violence on the day before and the day after Christmas". Retrieved from www.brethren.org, on 02/27/2021.

Cockayne, J and Walker S. (2016). "Fighting in conflict human trafficking: 10 Ideas for Action by the United Nations Security Council". Retrieved from http:/ INSECURITY,%20TRAFFICKING%20AND%20SEXUAL%20ABUSE/UNUReport_Pages.pdf, on 09/23/2020.

Daniel, S. (2013). *How We Saved Dasuki, IBB, From Assassins – DSS. Vanguard,* February 21.

Dauda, M, Ahmed M. Z. B. and Keling, M. F. (2017). 'Nigeria's Role and Its Peacekeeping Challenges in Africa: An Assessment.' European Journal of Social Sciences Studies. 2(3):46-71.

David, I. (2016). 'The Spectre of Terrorism and Nigeria's Industrial Development: A Multi-Stakeholder Imperative'.' African Journal of Criminology and Justice Studies, Vol.9, 1 May.

Denga, D. J. (1993). *Education at a Glance: From Cradle to Tomb,* Calabar: Rapid Educational Publishers Ltd.

DFID, (2005). *Girls Education: Towards a better future for all.* Geneva: Department of Development.

Don J. O. (2013). "Terrorism and Counter Terrorism in Nigeria: Theoretical Paradigms and

Lessons for Public Policy, Canadian Social Science," 9 (3). Retrieved from http:// www. cscanada.net.

Duez, (2002) 'De la définition à la labellisation: le terrorisme comme construction sociale', in Bannelier et al, (ed.), Responses to Terrorism or: Is There a Route from the 'Huntdown' in Afghanistan to Sustainable Globalization.

E. Hamilton(eds.) *The Handbook of Discourse Analysis*, pp.352–371. Oxford: Blackwell.

EDOREN, (2016). "Trends of inequality in access to schooling in Nigeria. Evidence from three DHS surveys". Retrieved from https://edorennigeria.files.wordpress. com/2014/07/ edoren-inequalities-in-access-to-chooling.pdf, on 09/13/2020.

Education for All (EFA), (2012). Global Monitoring Report.

Egbejule, E. (2018). "Deadly cattle raids in Zamfara: Nigeria's 'ignored' crisis" Aljazeera Africa Report. Retrieved from https://www.aljazeera.com/.../deadly-cat- tle-raids-zamfara-nigeria-crisis- 180819221942335.html, on 01/25/2020.

Egwu, S. (2016). *The political economy of rural banditry in contemporary Nigeria.* in Kuna, M.J and Ibrahim, J. (eds.). *Rural Banditry and Conflicts in Northern Nigeria, Abuja: Centre for Democracy and Development.*

Elumoye, D. (2021). "Bandits, kidnappers funding insurgency, says Fayemi". Retrieved from www.thisdaylive.com, on 04/07/2021.

Emmanuel, U. (2014) "Ohanaeze Youth Tackle Arewa over Call for Nigeria's Disintegration", ThisDay, Wednesday, July 23.

Encarta, (2009). "Terrorism". Retrieved on 28th August 2020.

English, R. (2009). *Terrorism: How to Respond.* Oxford: Oxford University Press.

Entman, R. M. (1993). 'Framing: Toward Clarification of a Fractured Paradigm', Journal of Communication. 43(4):51–58.

Epkins, H. N. (2008). 'How National Security Reporters Make Meaning of Terrorism Information Disseminated by the U.S. Government: An Extension of Mass Communication and Terrorism Theory.' Paper results presented for the second annual U.S. Department of Homeland Security University Network Summit, Washington, D.C.

Femi, T. (2011). 'The Challenges of Girl-Child Education and Alternative Jobs in Nigeria.' Corvinus Journal of Sociology and Social Policy 2(1): 101–121.

Fishman, M. (1980). *Manufacturing the news.* Austin: University of Texas Press

Freamon B. K. (2015). 'ISIS, Boko Haram and the human right to freedom from slavery under Islamic law'. Fordham International Law Journal 39 (2), 245-303.

Gaya, B.S. (2002). *The Challenges of Peacemaking and Peace Building in the Middle belt of Nigeria.* In E.E. Alemika & F. Okoye (Eds.). *Ethno-Religious Conflicts and Democracy in Nigeria: Challenges.* Kaduna: Human Right Monitor.

Gerald, M., and Cletrence J. B. (2013). *Nigerian Unity in the Balance.* USA: US Army War College Press.

Global Coalition for the Protection of Education from Attack (2018). "Education under Attack New York": GCPEA. Retrieved from http://eua2018.protectingeducation.org/, on 02/14/2021.

World Bank Group, (2016). "Basic Profile of Child Marriage in Nigeria," March. Retrieved from https://openknowledge.worldbank.org/bitstream/handle/10986/ 24547/, on 02/2020.

Global Coalition to Protect Education from Attack. (2019). "Problem". Retrieved from http://www.protectingeducation.org/problem, on 04/12/2021.

Goffman, E. (1974). *Frame Analysis: An Essay on the Organization of the Experience.* New York: Harper Colophon.

Guardian Newspaper, (2019), "Leah Sharibu: 2018 'Person of the Year", January 1.

Guardian Newspaper, (2021). 'Leah Sharibu gives birth to second baby in Boko Haram captivity." Retrieved from http://www.duradian_content_share.html, on 03/26/2021.

Gudaku, B. T. and Bulus, V. H. (2020). 'Islamic Movement of Nigeria (IMN) as Iran's Silhouette in Nigeria: An Examination of the Security and Diplomatic Contours and their Implications'. Albertine Journal of Philosophy, Vol. 4.

Gudaku, B. T. and Ogah M. A. (2019). 'Analyzing the Existing Threats and Potentials of the Myth and Reality of the Prediction of Possible Break-Up of Nigeria'. African Journal of Economics and Social Research 2(2): 91-103.

Gudaku, T. B. (2020). 'Contextualizing The Neo-Jihad in The Middle Belt Region Under the Disguised Veil of Herdsmen Attack'. Unpublished paper

Gudaku, T. B. (2021). 'An Inquisitive Discourse on the Vulnerability of Wrong Framing and the Rising Insecurity in Nigeria.' An Unpublished Work.

Hallahan, K. (1999). 'Seven Models of Framing: Implications for Public Relations'. Journal of Public Relations Research, 11(3), 205-242

Hassan H. A. (2015). 'Contending hegemony and the new security systems in Africa.' African Journal of Political Science and International Relations, Vol. 9(5): 159-169. DOI: 10.5897/AJPSIR2015.0772.

Health and Policy Training and Research Programme, (2028). 'Democratic Dividend Policy Brief, Number 2'. Retrieved from www.ui.edu.ng/hptrp, on 03/28/2021.

Herrmann, A. F. (2017). 'Hegemony.' The International Encyclopedia of Organizational Communication. 4(9): 1-6.

Hinshaw, D. and Parkinson, J., (2016). "The 10,000 Kidnapped Boys of Boko Haram", Wall Street Journal, 12 August. Retrieved from http:// www.wsj.com/articles/thc-kid- napped-boys-of-boko-haram-1471013062, on 04/27/2021.

Hoffman, B. (1998). *Inside Terrorism.* New York: Columbia University Press.

Hoffman. L. K. (2014). Who Speaks for the North? Politics and Influence in Northern Nigeria. London: Chatham House.

HRW, (2016). "They set the classrooms on Fire, Attacks on Education in Northeast Nigeria." Retrieved from https://www.hrw.org/sites/default/files/report_pdf/nigeria0416web.pdf, on 03/16/2021.

Human Right Watch, (2016). "Nigeria: A Year On, No Word on 300 Abducted Children, Government Response to Damasak Attacks Woefully Inadequate". Retrieved from https://www.hrw.org/news/2016/03/29/nigeria-year-no-word-300-abducted- children, on 08/28/2020.

Human Rights Watch. (2017). "Dreams Turned into Nightmares: Attacks on Students, Teachers, and Schools in Pakistan". Retrieved from https://www.hrw. org/report/2017/03/27/dreams-turned-nightmares/attacksstudents-teachers-and-schools-pakistan, 04/09/2021.

Human Rights, (2020). "Country Reports on Human Rights Practices for 2020". Retrieved from htpp://NIGERIA-2020-HUMAN-RIGHTS-REPORT.pdf, on 04/01/2021.

Hunwick, J. and Powell, E. T. (2002). *The African Diaspora in the Mediterranean lands of Islam.* London: Princeton.

Huruna, I. (2014). "Politics and People". Retrieved from http://www.ganji.com/haruna/haruna91.htm, on 03/03/2021.

Ibrahim, J. (2013). "Cultural Middle Belt and the marginalization of Nigerians." Retrieved from http://newsdairyonline.com/cultural-middle-belt-and-themarginalization-of-nigerians-by-jibrin-ibrahim, on 03/10/2021.

Ibrahim, J. (2016). "Nigeria: Rural Banditry - From the Crisis of Nomadism to State Crisis". Daily Trust. Retrieved from http://dailytrust.info/likked-60,000-cattle-rustled- in-2013, on 02/07/2020.

Ibuot, E. J. (2012). "Islamic Ideology, Western Rationalism and the Politics of Excluding the Feminine," Uchendu E. (ed.). New face of Islam in Eastern Nigeria and the Lake Chad Basin - Essays in Honour of Simon Ottenberg. Makurdi: Aboki Publishers

Idris, H. (2012). 'Gunmen sack four Maiduguri schools', Daily Trust, 29 February.

International Crisis Group Report (2020), 'Violence in Nigeria's North-west: Rolling Back the Mayhem'

International Crisis Group. (2010). 'Northern Nigeria: Background to Conflict', Africa Report, No. 168, 20 December.

Inwalomhe, D. (2021). "Abuse of women in IDPs." Guardian Newspapers. Retrieved from http://DUCATION%20AND%20GBV/IDPS%20AND%20GBV.html, on 03/02/2021.

IOM, (2017). 'Displacement Tracking Matrix: Round XVIII' Report-Nigeria, Abuja: IOM.

IRIN News (2013). 'Boko Haram attacks hit School attendance in Borno State.' Retrieved from http://www.irinnews.org/report/98032/boko-haram-attacks-hit-school- attendance-inborno-state, on 02/12/2021.

Ishaku, J. (2002). 'The Media and Ethno-Religious Conflicts in the Middle Belt of Nigeria.' In E.E. Alemika & F. Okoye (Eds.). Ethno-Religious Conflicts and Democracy in Nigeria: Challenges. Kaduna: Human Right Monitor.

Jaafar, J. (2018). "Rural banditry, urban violence and the rise of oligarchy by Professor Abubakar Liman". Retrieved from https://dailynigerian.com/rural-banditry-urban-violence-and-the-rise-of-oligarchyby-prof-abubakar-liman/, on 09/27/2020.

Jackson, R., Jarvis, L. Breen-Smyth, M. and Gunning, J. (2011). *Terrorism, a Critical Introduction.* Basingstoke: Palgrave Macmillan.

Johnston, N. (n.d.). 'Defining terrorism and insurgency: Beyond Morality.' Small War Journal.

Kamara, S. (2004). "Sierra Leone: Iranian Culture Centre to Reopen." Standard Times. April 6.

Kharbhih, H. (2010). 'Meghalaya model - combating human trafficking through a comprehensive framework that engages stakeholders.' Impulse NGO Network. 2010.

Kilcullen, D. (2013). *Out of the Mountains – the Coming Age of the Urban Guerilla.* New York: Oxford University Press.

Kiras, J. (2006). *Special Operations and Strategy from World War II to the War on Terrorism.* London: Routledge.

Koop, C. E. (1985). 'The surgeon general's workshop on violence and the public health'. Washington, DC: US Government Printing Office.

Kydd, A. H. and Walter, B. F. (2006) "The Strategies of Terrorism," International Security, 31(1): 49–80.

Lake Chad Basin Commission, (2018). "Regional Strategy for the Stabilization, Recovery & Resilience of the Boko Haram Affected Areas of the Lake Chad Basin Region," August.

Laqueur, W. (1976). *Guerrilla: A Historical and Critical Study.* Little, Brown: Boston.

Lepre, C. R. and Luther, C.A. (2007). 'The incorporation of terrorism coverage in academic Journalism programs.' Journalism and Mass Communication Educator, 61, 362-377.

Levitt, M. (2013). 'Hizballah & the Qods Forces in Iran's Shadow War with the West'. The Washington Institute of Near East Policy. January.

Lutz, (2002). "Was ist Terrorismus? Definitionen, Wandel, Perspektiven", in H.-J. Koch (Eds.). Terrorismus- Rechtsfragen der äußeren und inneren Sicherheit.

Lydon, G. and Hall, B. S. (20 Excavating Arabic sources for the history of slavery in Wester Africa. Retrieved from http://qt9jz5t0mn_noSplash_b1f784dc61eae087df- 023cfe5 affc0e2.pdf, on 04/08/2021.

Maclean, R. and Abrack, I. (2018). "Boko Haram kept one Dapchi girl who refused to deny her Christianity". The Guardian, Sunday, March 24.

Mahmood, O. S. (2017). 'More than propaganda A review of Boko Haram's public messages.' Institute for Security Studies, West African Report, 20 March.

Malunfashi, S. and Kaina, H. M. (2021). 'Inside Nigeria's Bandit camp,' VOA, February 27. Retrieved from http://www/BANDITARY/VOA.html, on 03/24/2021.

Mark, M. (2012). 'Boko Haram vows to fight until Nigeria establishes sharia law,' The Guardian, 27 January.

Martinez, E. (2013). 'Attacks On Education The impact of conflict and grave violations on children's futures', London; Save the Children Retrieved from https://www.savethechildren.org/content/dam/global/reports/education-and-childprotection/at- tacks-on-ed-2013.pdf, on 03/11/2021.

Mausi S. (2017) "Girls' Abductions a Last Straw for Nigerians, Government needs to get serious in protecting residents," Human Rights Watch, May 07. Retrieved from https://www.hrw.org/news/2014/05/07/girls-abductions-last-straw-nigerians, on 04/12/2021.

Mohammed, R. A. (2020), "Sokoto: Over 250 persons killed in 20 Deadly attacks," Daily Trust. Retrieved from https://dailytrust.com/how-bandits-killed-over-70-in-sokoto, on 03/12 /2021.

Mohammed, A. and Haruna, M. (2010). *Paradox of Boko Haram.* Abuja: Moving Image Limited.

Mohammed, A. U. (2013). 'Nigeria and the Boko Haram sect: adopting a better strategy for resolving the crisis.' Being a thesis Submitted to naval postgraduate School in partial fulfillment of the requirements for the degree of Mater of Arts Degree.

Mohammed, S. and Olagoke, B. (2021). "Father of released Zanfara schoolgirls: western education over for my daughters". Blueprint, Wednesday March 3.

Murdock, H. (2014). "Nigeria's Boko Haram Forces Victims to Fight, Kill," Voice of America, August 19.

Mustapha, A. R. (2014). 'Introduction: Interpreting Islam: Sufis, Salafists, Shiites and Islamists in Northern Nigeria'. Mustapha, A. R. (Ed.) Sects and Social Disorder- Muslim identities and Conflict in Northern Nigeria. Woodbridge: James and Currey.

Mvendaga, T. L., Ifeanyichukwu, A. J. and Apine, N. (2014). Problems and Challenges of Girl-Child Education in Nigeria: The Situation of Kalgo Local Government Area (L.G.A) of Kebbi State. Journal of Research & Method in Education (JRME), 4 (4), 01-05.

National Education Data Survey (2010). Retrieved from https://www.eddataglobal. org/household/index.cfm?fuseaction=show-DatasetDir&A2=NG, on 08/11/2020.

NBS (2017). National Survey. Abuja: National Bureau of Statistics.

Nigeria Partnership for Education Project (2015), Project Appraisal Document (PAD).

Nine-Eleven Commission, (2014). 'Final Report of the National Commission on Terrorist Attacks on the United States'. Washington, DC: Government Printing Office.

Nizzero, M. (2018). 'Ungoverned spaces. Why some jihadist groups engage in public service delivery more than others'. Retrieved from http://www./ibei_studentpaper42_162029.pdf, on 12/28/2020.

Njoku, A.O. and Nwafor, P.I. (2005). 'Nigeria's External Relations'. Enugu: Redeemed Printing and Publishing Company.

Norris, P., Kern, M., and Just M. R. (2003). *Framing terrorism.* In P. Norris, M.R. Just, and M. Kern (Eds.). *Framing terrorism: The news media, the government, and the public* (pp. 3-25). New York: Routledge.

Obasi, E. (1997), "Structural Adjustment and Gender Access to Education in Nigeria". Gender and Education, 19, 161 – 177.

OCHA, (2017). 'Humanitarian Needs Overview: Nigeria', January 13.

Odafe, G. (2003). The Middle Belt in Nigeria's Retrogression. The Gadfly Magazine, 4 (6), 22-23.

Odo, A. (2013). "SSS Busts Alleged Iran-Linked 'Spy Network". Daily Trust, February 21.

Odula, T. (2013). "Kenya Court Sentences 2 Iranians to Life in Jail". Associated Press, May 6.

Office to Monitor and Combat Trafficking in Persons (2016). Civilian Security, Democracy, and Human Rights: Civilian Security, Democracy, and Human Rights.

Retrieved from http:/INSECURITY,%20TRAFFICKING%20AND%20SEXUAL%20 ABUSE/259303.pdf, on 03/19/2020.

OHCHR, (2008). "Rape: Weapon of war." Retrieved from http://www.ohchr.org/en/newsevents/ pages/rapeweaponwar.aspx, on 02/09/2021.

Ojukwu, C.C, (2011). "Terrorism, Foreign and Human Rights Concern in Nigeria." Journal of Sustainable Development in Africa, 13 (4), 22-31.

Okocha, M. (2009). 'Parental Attitudes towards Vocational Education.' Edu (LASSON) Journal of Counseling; 2 (1): 81 – 89.

Okoli, A. L. C. and Ugwu, A. C. (2019). 'Of Marauders and Brigands: Scoping the Threat of Rural Banditry in Nigeria's North West.' Brazilian Journal of African Studies. 4 (8), 201-222.

Okoli, A.C. and Okpaleke, F.N. (2014). "Banditry and crisis of public safety in Nigeria: issues in national security strategies," European Scientific Journal 10(4): 350–362.

Okoli, C. A. I. (2021). 'What can be done to fight banditry in Northern Nigeria.' Retrieved from http://www/BANDITARY/RELIEFWEB.html, on 03/15/2021.

Oladosu, A. (2007). 'Education reforms in Nigeria: implications for private Arabic school.'

A paper presented at the National Conference on Education Reforms in Nigeria: Past, Present, and future organized by the faculty of Education, University of Ilorin, from 25th -28th May.

Olaniyan, A. (2018). "Once Upon a Game Reserve: Sambisa and the Tragedy of a Forested Landscape." Environment & Society Portal, no. 2. Rachel Carson Center for Environment and Society. doi.org/10.5282/rcc/8176.

Olukoya, S. (2021). 'Hundreds of Nigerian Schoolgirls taken in mass abduction.' Associated Press, March 1.

Onyebuchi, E. (2020), "Bandits now move in the north from house to house with AK47",

Osimen, G.U, Akinwunmi, A. A., Adetula, S. L. (2015). 'Peace Keeping Role of Nigeria in Sub-Sahara Africa.' International Journal of Research in Humanities and Social Studies. 2(10), 26-34.

OUSD (2007). 'Ungoverned Areas and Threats from Safe Havens,' Washington, DC: US Department of Defense.

Outhred, R. and Turner, F. (2020). 'Prospective evaluation of GPE's country-level support to education.' Final Report - Year 2. January.

Peters, V. V., and Akpan B. S. (2017). 'Girl – Child Education: Implication for Women and National Development.' International Journal of Research Development, 3 (4), 23-30.

Philips, B. J. (2015). 'What Is a Terrorist Group? Conceptual Issues and Empirical Implications.' Terrorism and Political Violence, 27, 225-242.

Pinto, V. C. (2014). 'Exploring the interplay between Framing and Securitization theory: The case of the Arab Spring protests in Bahrain.' Rev. Bras. Polít. Int. 57 (1): 162- 176.

Piombo, J. R. (2007). 'Terrorism and U. S. Counter-Terrorism Programs in Africa: An Overview,' Strategic Insights, 6 (1) 34-41.

Protocol to Prevent, Suppress and Punish Trafficking in Persons Especially Women and Children, supplementing the United Nations Convention against Transnational Organized Crime, 15 November 2000, Article 3, para (a).

Quénivet, N. (2005). 'The World after September 11: Has It Really Changed? The European Journal of International Law' 16 (3): 561–577. doi: 10.1093/ejil/chi131

Reese, S. D. (2001b). Framing public life: A bridging model for media research. In S.

D. Reese, O. H. Gandy, and A.E. Grant (Eds.), Framing public life. (pp. 7-31). Mahwah, NJ: Erlbaum.

Reserve, Borno State, Nigeria. International Journal of Research in Agriculture and Forestry, 2 (2), 1-5.

Reuters, (2013). 'Nigeria Seizes $9.9 Heroin Shipment from Iran.' November 19.

Ridgeon, L. (2012). *Shi'a Islam and Identity: Religion, Politics and Change in the Global*

Muslim Community. New York: I. B. Tauris.

Russo, N. F. and Pirlott, A. (2006). 'Gender-Based Violence: Concepts, Methods, and Findings.' Ann. N.Y. Acad. Sci. 1087: 178–205.

Rychnovska, D. (2014). 'Securitization and the Power of Threat Framing.' Perspectives 22 (2), 9-32.

Sagir, M. (2017). 'The Challenges of Counter Terrorism Enforcement in Nigeria.' Retrieved from http://www.newsdiaryonline.com, on 03/02/2021.

Samuel, M. (2019). 'Economics of Terrorism in Lake Chad Basin,' Institute for Security Studies, July 10.

Sauer, N. (2019). 'Lake Chad Not Shrinking, but Climate Is Fueling Terror Groups: Report,' Climate Home News, May 16.

Scheufele, D. A. (2000). Agenda-setting, priming, and framing revisited: Another look at cognitive effects of political communication. Mass Communication and Society, 3, 297-316.

Schmid, A. (2004). 'Terrorism-the definitional problem.' Case W. Res. J. Int'l L., 36, 375.

Schmid, A. P., Jongman, A. J. and Stohl. M. L. (1988). 'Political Terrorism: A New Guide to Actors, Authors, Concepts, Data Bases, Theories, and Literature.' Amsterdam: North-Holland Pub.

Schmidt, P. A. and Jongman, A. I. (1988). *Political Terrorism SWIDOC, Amsterdam and Transaction Books.*

Shilgba, L.K. (2013). The Middle Belt Federation in British Nigeria. Retrieved from http://www.nairaland.com/674760/towards-true-federalism-middle-belt,on 03/09/2021.

Sklar, B.C. (1963). Nigerian Political Parties in Emergent African Nations. Lagos: NOK Publishers. Slavery Convention, 1927.

Sorel, (2002). 'Existe-t-il une définition universelle du terrorisme?', in K. Bannelier et al. (eds.), Le droit international face au terrorisme.

Stevens, D., and Vaughan-Williams (2014). 'Citizens and security threats: issues, perceptions and consequences beyond the national frame.' B. J. pol. S (46): 146-175.

Sule, A. M. (2013). 'Nigeria's participation in peacekeeping operations.' Being a Thesis Presented in Partial Completion of the Rcquirements of the Certificate-of-Training in United Nations Peace Support Operation.

Sunday Trust, (2012). "The Lost Glory of Rugu Forest." Retrieved from http://Rugu. html, on 05/21/2020.

Sweene, A. (2015). "Iran Summons Nigerian Envoy over Zaria Bloodbath". Retrieved from https://www.naij.com/667287-iran-outraged-nigeria-zaria-bloodbath.html, on 08/06/2020.

Taiwo, J. and Olugbode, M. (2009). "Nigeria News Update: Mohammed Yusuf Killed while in Custody," Pan-African News Wire, July 31. Retrieved from http://panafri- cannews. blogspot.com/2009/07/nigerianews-update-mohammed-yusuf.html, on 03/21/2021.

Tattersall, N. (2010). "Weapons Seized in Nigeria Came from Iran: Shipping Company". Reuters, October 30.

Taylor, A.J. (2016). 'Thoughts on the nature and consequences of ungoverned spaces.' SAIS Review of International Affairs, 36 (1). pp. 5-15.

The Guardian, 19 April 2013, 'French family seized in Cameroon by suspected Boko Haram Islamists freed' via http://www.theguardian.com/world/2013/apr/19/ french-family-kidnapped-cameroon-freed accessed 01/09/2014.

The Humanitarian (2018). "Zamfara: Nigeria's wild northwest". Retrieved from http:// www. thenewhumanitarian.org/news-feature/2018/09/13/zamfara-nigeria-s-wild- northwest, on 02/12/2020.

The Nation, (2019). 'Government, El-Zakzaky, Shiites and the Law.' Tuesday, August 6.

ThisDayLive. Retrieved from https://www.thisdaylive.com/index.php/2020/11/26/ bandits-now-move-in-the-north-from-house-to-house-with-ak47-says-sultan, on 02/23/2021.

Thurston, A. (2016). 'The disease is unbelief': Boko Haram's religious and political worldview.' The Brookings Project on U.S. Relations with the Islamic World. Analysis Paper, No. 22, January.

Uchegbu, A. (2021). 'Leah Sharibu: Shame of a republic.' DailySun, Thursday, March 25.

Ugwumba, E.U. and Odom, T.C. (2014). 'Boko Haram Insurgency: A Peril to Achievement of Education for all in Nigeria.' International Journal of Education Learning and Development, 3(1): 1-11

UKAID (2012). 'Gender in Nigeria Report 2012: Improving the Lives of Girls and Women in Nigeria,' London: UKAID.

Ukwu, J. (2021). "UK Govt Says No Partnership Will Resolve Nigeria's Security Situation." Retrieved from www.Naij.com, on 02/23/2021.

UNDP (2015). Gender Equality Index 2015. New York: UNDP.

UNDP, (2018). "Perspectives from Local Communities on Stabilization and Building Peace in the Lake Chad Basin," May.

UNFPA, (2016). "Preparedness and Response to the Rescued Girls." Retrieved from http://reliefweb.int/report/nigeria/unfpa-preparedness-and-response-rescued-girls, on 02/24/2020.

UNICEF (2013). "Condemns killings in school attacks in northeast Nigeria," 6 July. Retrieved from http://www.unicef.org/media/media_69782.html, on 02/19/2021.

UNICEF, (2017). "Making Schools Safer and Students more Confident," September 22. Retrieved from https://www.unicef.org/nigeria/media_11644.html, on 09/30/2020.

UNICEF. (2005) "Education". Retrieved from https://www.unicef.org/nigeria/children_1937.html, on 03/17/2021.

United Nations Children Education Fund (UNICEF) (2012). "Goal: Promote Gender Equality and Empower Women." Retrieved from http//www.unicef.org/mdg/gender/html, on 03/03/2021.

United Nations. (1995). The United Nations Fourth World Conference on Women: Platform for action. Retrieved from http://www.un.org/womenwatch/daw/beijing/platform/girl.htm, on 02/16/2021.

UNOG, (2017). "Regular Press Briefing: Attack against primary school in Nigeria," December 1. Retrieved from https://www.unog.ch/80256EDD006B9C2E/(httpNewsByYear_en)/, on 08/28/2020.

US Department of State (2016). Trafficking in Persons Report 2016. Washington DC:

US DOS. Adepelumi, P. (2015). 'The Root Causes of Human Trafficking in Nigeria.'

High-level Event on the U.N. Trust Fund for Victims of Trafficking in Persons 13th U.N. Crime Congress, Doha, Qatar 13th of April.

Utibe, T. M. (2016). 'Domestic Terrorism and Its Impacts on Nigerian State: An Analysis of Boko Haram Insurgency.' International Journal of Innovative Research and Studies 5(1). Retrieved from www.ijirs.com, on 04/27/2021.

Uzuegbu-Wilson, E. (2016). "A Critical Review of Attacks on Schools in Nigeria: Lessons Learned." Retrieved from https://ssrn.com/abstract=3456225, on 09/06/2020.

Van Dijk, T. A. (2001) 'Critical Discourse Analysis', in Deborah Schiffrin–Deborah Tannen–Heidi.

Van Krieken, P. J. (2002). 'Terrorism and the International Legal Order with Special Reference to the U.N.,' the EU and Cross-Border Aspects.

Vanguard, (2011). "Arms Shipment: Nigeria Trial Will Expose Iran Gun-running".

January 19. Vanguard, (2013). "Suspect Alleges Plot to Kill Saudi Ambassador to Nigeria". August 3.

Wæver, O. (1995) 'Securitization and Desecuritization'. In D.R. Lipschutz (Eds.) On Security, 46–86. New York: Columbia University Press.

Warner, J. and Matfess, H. (2017). "Exploding Stereotypes: The Unexpected Operational and Demographic Characteristics of Boko Haram's Suicide Bombers," Combating Terrorism Center at West Point, August. Retrieved from https://ctc.usma.edu/ report-exploding-stereotypes-the-unexpectedoperational-and-demographic-charac- teristics-of-boko-harams-suicide-bombers/, on 02/27/2020.

WEF, (2016). "The Global Competitiveness Report 2016–2017". Retrieved from https://www.weforum.org/reports/the-global-competitiveness-report-2016-2017-1/, on 03/03/2020.

West African Network for Peacebuilding (2020). "Addressing Armed Banditry in the North-West Region of Nigeria: Exploring the Potentials of a Multi-Dimensional

Conflict Management Approach. " Retrieved from http://www.BANDITARY/POLICY_BRIEF_ON_ARMED_BANDITRY_IN_NIGERIA_-_18022020.pdf, on 02/23/2020.

Wilkinson, P. (2006). *Terrorism versus Democracy: Terrorism, Insurgency and asymmetrical conflicts,* London: Routledge.

Wood, E. J. (2006). 'Variation in Sexual Violence during War.' Politics & Society, 34 (3),307-342.

World Bank, (2014). "Nigeria economic report. Nigeria economic report; no. 2." Washington, DC: World Bank Group. Retrieved from http:// documents.worldbank.org/curated/en/337181468100145688/Nigeria-economic-report, on 11/02/2020.

World Bank, (2015). "Governance, Accountability, and Finance. Analysis in the Ba- sic Education Sector in Nigeria." Retrieved from https://openknowledge.worldbank.org/bitstream/handle/10986/23683/Governance0and0on0sector0in0Nigeria.pdf?se-quence=1, on 01/19/2021.

Yilmaz, S. (2010). 'State, Power, and Hegemony. International Journal of Business and Social Science' 1(3): 192-205.

YouTube, 11 January 2012, 'Message to Jonathan from Abubaker Shekau' (translation) via http://www. youtube.com/watch?v=eNg73vN86K8.

Yusuf, A. Y. M. (2008). Hadhihi 'Aqidatuna wa-Manhaj Da'watina (likely Maiduguri, 2008).

Zenn, J and Pearson, E. (2014). 'Women, Gender and the evolving tactics of Boko Haram.' Journal of Terrorism Research, 5(1): 46-57.

Zenn, J. (2013). 'The Islamic Movement of Nigeria and Iranian Intelligence Activities in Nigeria.' CTC Sentinel, 6 (10).